When Harry Met Minnie

WHEN HARRY MET MINNIE

A TRUE STORY OF LOVE AND FRIENDSHIP

MARTHA TEICHNER

THORNDIKE PRESS
A part of Gale, a Cengage Company

GALE
A Cengage Company

**LIBRARY OF CONGRESS CIP DATA ON FILE.
CATALOGUING IN PUBLICATION FOR THIS BOOK
IS AVAILABLE FROM THE LIBRARY OF CONGRESS.**

ISBN-13: 978-1-4328-8951-7 (hardcover alk. paper)

Published in 2021 by arrangement with Celadon Books

Printed in Mexico
Print Number: 01   Print Year: 2021

*For Minnie and Harry and,
of course, Carol*

ONE:
CHANCE ENCOUNTER

On most Saturday mornings, I leave for the Union Square farmers market early, when Manhattan feels as if it belongs just to me. I need to go there every week I'm in town. That need has less to do with fruits and vegetables, cheese and flowers, more to do with a New York state of mind. I need the brightness of day, the emptiness of the streets, the license to look at the city, listen to it, when it's still sleepy, just waking up. I need the weather, season to season. And I need at least one dog walking along beside me, even better, two, as I push my grocery cart east, across town, and then back. Without a dog or two beside me, I feel incomplete. I catch myself talking to one or the other even if they're not there and then feel like an idiot.

I know the route so well I can walk it in my mind. I can conjure it up in winter when the light is thin and gray, the color of old

stone buildings, or in the summer when the morning sun blinds me as I head east on Twenty-second Street. In the spring, when cherry blossoms make the sidewalks look like natural parade floats arched in pink pompoms, and in the fall, when West Chelsea brownstones dress up for Halloween.

As I walk, I love to look at the ornate facades of what passed for skyscrapers a century or so ago reflected as mocking, funhouse distortions of themselves on the new glass boxes around them. I wonder when I see the row of stone lion heads above the windows of the Old Navy store what sort of past lives the building had. I always stop and get out a dollar bill well before I reach, propped against his wall, the homeless man who likes dogs. He's there most Saturday mornings and has asked me to follow him on YouTube rapping.

On each block, there are a hundred things to notice: a man in a bright orange shirt riding a bike no-handed, slaloming down Broadway singing, a stretch of sidewalk laid with worn squares of slate shiny after being hosed down, giant blow-up soccer balls outside bars during the World Cup. For dogs: garbage and dropped pizza slices and little rivers to be sniffed and other dogs.

In my opinion, the Union Square farmers

market is reason enough to live in New York City. On Saturdays in the summer, there are more than sixty stalls. Chefs, accompanied by helpers pushing giant wheelbarrows or carts, cruise for the best strawberries or exotic kale or the tastiest heirloom tomatoes to turn into somebody's birthday or date-night meal. The market is about possibility.

When I began going to the Union Square farmers market in 1994, not long after I moved to New York, Piggy went with me. My first bull terrier, he was a brindle, meaning he looked like a white dog wearing a blackish-brownish striped jacket that was too small. I got him as a crazy puppy, while I was the CBS News correspondent in South Africa. I was transferred to London and eventually back to the United States. He came along. Making our way to and from the farmers market, a three-mile round-trip, was more like waterskiing or chariot driving than walking. I accompanied him. He didn't accompany me. We went his way, and the route was different every week. He considered the farmers market one vast treat opportunity. I'd buy him apples and pears, plums and peaches, whatever was in season, whatever was heaped high on tables or in crates on the ground.

■ ■ ■ ■

Going to the farmers market with Piggy, I always felt as if we were up to something together. It was fun. At some point, I couldn't say when, our weekly expeditions became important to me.

On Saturday mornings, Piggy and I would get to the market just as it was opening, to avoid crowds, and in the summer, to avoid the heat. There, we would usually meet another bull terrier, Zeke, and his owners, Mike and Julia. More than twenty-five years later, I still see Mike and Julia every Saturday. After Zeke came Simon. After Simon came Sunny, a brindle like Piggy, but bigger and much, much better behaved. Likewise, after Piggy came Goose, a scoundrel and a thief if there ever was one, and then Minnie joined us. A sorry-looking rescue when I got her, she transformed into a sleek glamour-puss, full of attitude.

Bull terriers are not that common a breed. To see one is fairly unusual, but if you went to the Union Square farmers market on a Saturday morning leading up to the time the events in this story took place, you might have seen as many as four. Sunny; Seamus, a wildly exuberant miniature who looked like a junior version of Sunny; Minnie and Goose, that is until Goose had to be put down. Then there were three.

The Saturday market is loaded with dogs, all kinds. But I have to say, tourists go crazy at the sight of a whole gathering of bull terriers standing together and have to take pictures. The jam ladies always smiled and waved as I went by with Minnie. So did the NYC rooftop-honey man. A woman with streaks of pink in her hair always knelt to pet her. We always seemed to run into her near the goat-cheese stall. Annie, a seventy-something-year-old psychologist who always wears a baseball cap, wanders the market feeding her favorite dogs fistfuls of treats, regaling their owners with stories about her various preoccupations, which include NASCAR races and how to be happy. Where I buy apples, the man in charge of the stand always used to laugh when Goose would help himself to a big juicy one from a crate on the ground. I'd offer to pay, but most of the time the man would wave me away. When Goose couldn't make it all the way to the market anymore, the man asked me where he was. If the weather was really bad, if it was too hot or too cold or raining or snowing, and Minnie refused to go with me, I felt invisible. I've been a correspondent

11

with CBS News for more than forty years. Six million or more people watch *CBS Sunday Morning,* where I've worked since 1993. I get recognized every day no matter where I am, but the funny thing is, when I go to the Union Square market dogless, it's as if I don't exist, which has advantages, sometimes. I like being a bit player in the happy weekly street theater that takes place among the fruits and vegetables and flowers, in which the four-legged actors, not the two-legged ones, are the stars.

July 23, 2016, started out the way most summer Saturdays did. It was warm, sunny. Six months after Goose's death, Minnie still didn't want to go on walks. She still missed him, still looked for him, still seemed sad, so getting her to the market took some convincing. Bull terriers are exceptionally good at refusing. They're genetically wired to be stubborn, so we carried on our argument until I tugged and nudged her to the end of our block. We crossed the street, and she gave in.

Sometime in early 2007, Minnie was dumped to die. She wore no collar or anything else to identify her. She had just had puppies, so maybe a puppy mill had used her for breeding and then gotten rid of her. Who knows what happened to the puppies? It was cold, days around twenty degrees, nights around ten. How she survived is a miracle. She was picked up in a rough area east of East Flatbush in Brooklyn by New York's Animal Care & Control dogcatchers and taken to the big ACC shelter not far away. Thousands of animals are destroyed there every year.

On a Saturday early that February, a reporter from *Rolling Stone* magazine, Coco McPherson, embedded herself as a volunteer at the shelter hoping to write an article about how its kill policy worked and why it was so difficult to find out which animals were docketed to die and when. She'd adopted a succession of unwanted pit bulls and multiple cats from shelters. She was surprised to find a purebred bull terrier at such a place. The workers had named the dog Lil' Kim, after the rapper who went to prison for lying about her friends' involvement in a shooting. The poor thing was a wreck, so emaciated she looked like a skeleton, all the bones in her tail showing, all her ribs. Underneath the filth, she was white. She'd had a bath, but this was grime that would have to grow out. A broad stripe of yellow fur ran down the middle of her back, the result of malnutrition. Because she had given birth so recently, her tits still hung down. After a week at the shelter living on borrowed time, she charmed Coco McPherson. "Spay her, and I'll pick her up next week. She's too cute to kill."

The same day, Coco went into the Barking Zoo, her neighborhood pet-accessory store in Chelsea, and mine. She asked the clerks if they knew anybody who might be willing to adopt a bull terrier. She had three dogs and two cats and couldn't manage another animal in her apartment. A woman behind the counter said, "Oh, we know a woman with a big, sweet bull terrier. Maybe she'd take her." On weekends, I typically walked Goose to the Barking Zoo and bought him a big jerky treat, like a mother taking her child for an ice cream. It was a bribe, a way to make him get some exercise, so he wouldn't just stand around refusing to move away from the front stoop. On Sunday, the day after Coco McPherson had been in, I convinced Goose it would be worth his while to make the trip. The woman who rang up his treat said, "Oh, am I glad to see you." Suspicious, I responded, "Why? I was in here yesterday." She told me about the bull terrier in the shelter and asked if I would consider taking her. I replied, "I don't want a second dog. One is enough." She asked me to think about it and said she would have Coco McPherson call me. I could discuss it with her.

I'm a soft touch. I agreed to "foster" the dog. The following Saturday at noon, I arrived at the Barking Zoo with Goose. Coco brought the rescue dog. In the crowded, busy store, the two of them sized each other up. Goose was more interested in treats than in this other animal, who seemed shell-shocked and too scared to be interested in anything at all. Coco bought her a sweater. We led the two dogs to my apartment, then decided to take the rescue dog to the vet, whose clinic was at the end of my block, a five-minute walk unless you're walking a bull terrier. After a week and a half of being fed in the shelter, she weighed just barely thirty-four pounds. Her appropriate weight is around fifty pounds. Her spaying had been botched, so she had a serious infection. A thousand dollars later, I took her home. I think I had already decided to keep her, rationalizing the decision by saying to myself that it would be unfair to put her through yet another rupture. She had suffered enough. I decided to rename her Minnie, not Mini like the car or because she was small, but Minnie, as in Mouse.

She just seemed like a Minnie.

At first, she seemed terrified to eat. She would stand over her bowl rigid, staring at it. I found myself trying to imagine her story, to figure out the mystery of her past. Minnie immediately took over my laundry bin. It's tubular, maybe two and a half feet high, and is made out of stiffened canvas reinforced with wires. She tipped it over and burrowed inside with my dirty clothes. The first time, before I'd realized she was inside, I saw it convulse suddenly. I jumped and then saw her. Every time I ironed, she sat under the ironing board. She liked women but was afraid of some men. I could imagine a half dozen scenarios, given those clues.

Every day she tried to kill Goose. He was a generous, sweet boy who was happy to welcome a companion. Minnie would stare at him, and everybody else for that matter, with a wild, wary devil-dog look. She figured out quickly that I was the key to her well-being, to meals and warmth and attention. She would attack Goose whenever he tried to get near me. When bull terriers fight, it can be dangerous. They're strong. After multiple bloody dogfights, I worried that I would have to give her up. I didn't want to think about shunting her off to someone else, but I didn't want a dead dog or to be seriously injured myself trying to separate the two of them.

It troubled me that Minnie never seemed to learn her name. No matter how many times I repeated it or how loudly I said it, she failed to react. She seemed to be startled and would instinctively snarl and lunge if anyone came up behind her. Soon I suspected she might be deaf and had her tested. Sure enough. It explained a lot about her behavior. Learning that she couldn't hear at all made me marvel again at how she'd managed to survive in a not-so-nice part of New York City before being picked up by the dogcatchers. How had she avoided getting hit by a car?

When the fights were at their worst, I was working on a *CBS Sunday Morning* story about a man named Bill Berloni, who trains shelter dogs for Broadway shows and is the behaviorist for the New York Humane Society. He evaluates new arrivals at the Humane Society shelter to determine whether they're ready for placement and what sort of home each needs. I told him about Minnie and how afraid I was I'd have to give her up. His advice: establish a hierarchy. In the Teichner pack, I had to be Number One, the Alpha. Then came Goose. Minnie came last. He suggested physically

17

positioning Minnie behind Goose in the kitchen when treats were being given out or when they got their meals. When we headed out on walks, I had to arrange to go out the door first, then Goose, then Minnie. If she snarled at Goose, my instructions were to reprimand her and put her in her crate. If she looked at me before picking a fight, I was supposed to praise her. With Bill Berloni's help, within a month, the fights stopped.

Minnie became devoted to Goose. He was her guide and eventually her sneaky partner in crime. When she arrived, she wasn't housebroken. Goose taught her to go outside. She wouldn't walk without him. Every day, when I got home, Goose would find a way to tip over my handbag on the floor. It didn't matter how high up I put it, he'd get it. With the contents spread out under my dining table, he'd carefully hunt for cough drops. He wasn't interested in the pens or my hairbrush or checkbook. He loved cough drops. Given my line of work, I always had cough drops in my bag. Broadcasters tend to need them. Minnie would appear, take some for herself, then disappear, leaving Goose to get in trouble for piracy. She usually hid in my bed. As soon as the bed is made, Minnie unmakes it. She snorts, paws at the sheets ferociously, tosses back the duvet with her nose, then buries herself underneath the covers. I find her wrapped up as if she were in a cocoon or else sleeping with her head on a pillow, looking innocent enough to suggest that she should be a saint. It took a year, but Skinny Minnie filled out and became very grand indeed in the jeweled collar I felt she had to have, convinced as she was that she was a glamorous movie star or maybe a princess.

For nearly half his life, Goose had serious heart issues. By the time I had to have him put to sleep, at the beginning of 2016, he was taking half a dozen different medications. He could barely walk. We were in South Carolina when he collapsed. I took him to the vet, but she misdiagnosed or underestimated his condition.

I took him home. Seeing him suffer was terrible. Minnie would sniff Goose from time to time and try to make me pay attention to her. She watched at the door as I struggled to get Goose into the car when I took him back to the vet. Only later, when I came home without him, when Minnie realized he was gone, did she react. She looked everywhere for him, not just in South Carolina but once we got back to New York. She checked under the stairs down to the garden, where he always went to pee, and in the kitchen by his water bowl. She sniffed his bed, his toys, his sweaters, not just once but every day, again and again. She seemed scared, vulnerable, the little deaf dog who had lost her companion of nine years, her protector, her good luck charm. Getting her to go for walks became an ordeal. She didn't want to eat. She stopped being a cheeky, joyful flirt. Goose died in January. Well into the summer, Minnie was still despondent. Dogs do mourn. I was afraid she would be permanently depressed. I decided I needed to find an older, male bull terrier to keep her company and kept checking all the rescue websites, but none materialized.

I told myself I was trying to help *her,* but the truth is, I was just as sad as Minnie. I missed my Goosey desperately. I got him from a breeder in North Carolina in the fall of 2002. On the day I picked him up, when he was three months old, my cousin went with me. She gave him a woolly fleece toy shaped rather like a gingerbread man. He immediately put it between his front paws and began kneading it and sucking one of its arms, as if he were nursing. Over time, the arm stretched out, so it looked a little grotesque. Goosey never outgrew sucking on his fleece man. He wore out many. He and Minnie played tug-of-war with a few and tore them to pieces. Often on Sunday mornings, while I watched *CBS Sunday Morning,* I sewed them up with whatever color thread came in all the little hotel sewing kits I had collected in my travels, so most of Goose's fleece men had strange red or blue or gray Frankenstein scars. After he died, for months I took the last of his fleece men to bed with me and clung to him. I packed him in my suitcase when I traveled on assignment, just to have him with me in whatever unfamiliar hotel room I checked into late at night. I still have him on a bench near my bed.

So, on that July 23, as Minnie and I made our way to the Union Square market, some of the bright, Saturday-morning pleasure I always felt was dulled by how much we still missed Goose. We had no idea what we were about to walk into, that our lives were about to be transformed, that a chance encounter would soon set in motion a sad and wonderful New York story . . . this story.

It was eight-thirty, and that mattered, as it turned out. I had bought my flowers already. Minnie and I were standing at the northeast corner of the market, for anybody who knows the place, between the Stokes Farm stand and Cato Corner Cheese. I was talking to Mike and Julia, Sunny's people. Minnie was ignoring Sunny, as she usually did. A couple of other acquaintances had stopped to chat, too.

A stocky, bearded man with tattoos on his arms approached us. He had a large, fluffy golden retriever with him. I recognized them from walking with Goose and Minnie early in the morning in the park along the Hudson River at Chelsea Piers. Once, big steamships docked at Chelsea Piers. Now it's a big sports complex surrounded by grassy areas and bike paths. It had been a couple of years since I'd seen the man and his dog there. Goose could still make it to the river then. For months this man and I had talked, carrying on long, meaty conversations some days, just saying hello other times. I'd go away on assignment. When I got back, he'd be there. I don't think he ever knew my name or I his, but we knew each other's dogs' names. Typical among New York dog-walking friends. Then, suddenly, he disappeared. Another Chelsea Piers dog-walking acquaintance told me he'd moved way uptown. Now here he was at the farmers market.

"Where's Goose?" he asked, pointing down at Minnie. I told him. I said that

Goose's heart had failed and mine was broken, that Minnie was inconsolable, that I'd been looking for an older, male bull terrier to be Minnie's companion but so far hadn't found one to adopt.

He rummaged in his pocket and pulled out his phone. He swiped the screen, paused, then did it again, shaking his head, then again. "Wait," he said, as he found what he was looking for. He showed me a photograph of Goose and Minnie in their winter coats. The two dogs looked stubbornly uninterested, not just in having their pictures taken, but uninterested in walking, uninterested in anything, as only bull terriers can be. I laughed, thinking . . . unlike your big, eager golden. "Remind me what your dog's name is." "Teddy," he answered. "Remember, I took this picture to send to my friend Carol, who has a bull terrier?" By this time, he and I were by ourselves, our dogs at our feet. The others had drifted off to do their shopping. "Vaguely, it's coming back to me," I replied. I remembered weeks of standing in the cold dressed in so many layers of fleece and down, I felt as if I were wearing an extra person or could pass for the Michelin Man.

The chunky ring of keys hanging from a heavy chain in his back pocket, the tattoos, and the shaved head contradicted his careful speech, his resonant voice. His beard and mustache were carefully trimmed, sculpted almost, very nineteenth-century gentleman. I'd known him for several years but didn't know him at all. Who was he? Who was his friend Carol with the bull terrier?

When I go to the market, I take my iPod, which has a built-in FM radio. I hang it around my neck on a lanyard and listen to NPR's *Weekend Edition* starting at eight o'clock. I'm a professional news junkie. I have to be. I stood there with an earbud stuck in one ear, the other one hanging down, half listening to the news, half speculating about this man I hadn't seen in a long time. I half heard him say, "Carol is dying of liver cancer. She's desperate to find a home for Harry, her dog. He's eleven and a half. She's more concerned about him than she is about herself. He's got some issues, but he's very sweet. Would you take him?"

"What?" Suddenly, I was paying attention. "Say that again." He repeated what he'd just told me, but this time added, "Nobody wants him. The vet has warned her she should be prepared to have him put down. Would you take him?"

"Well . . ." I felt startled and a little light-

24

headed. I knew, I really did, that something big and important had just begun. "Well, maybe, if he and Minnie get along. Possibly." I suggested getting the two dogs together to meet. He said he had a car and could drive Harry and Carol to my apartment. In spite of the years we'd been acquainted, all those months we'd spent talking, we had to introduce ourselves. Stephen Miller Siegel . . . Martha Teichner. When I go to the market, I take my passport and all my credit cards out of my wallet and only carry the cash I need and one business card for identification. I handed it to him. He looked at it and took in that I work for CBS News, that I am a correspondent on a show he watches regularly. When I walk my dogs in the morning or go to the farmers market, I look more like a bag lady than the person people see on television. I wear sloppy clothes and no makeup, but even so, people recognize me, often just because they know my voice. Evidently, walking our dogs at Chelsea Piers, Stephen never made the connection, which is fine with me. He gave me his card and said he would contact Carol.

We went our separate ways. It was a five-minute exchange. That's it. If I'd been standing somewhere else; if I'd been there at eight forty-five instead of eight-thirty; if it had been raining, and Minnie and I had stayed home, Stephen would not have seen us. In more than two decades of going to the Union Square market practically every Saturday morning, year-round, never, not once, had I ever seen him there before.

Chance had just made us characters in a remarkable story, a very New York story, about friendship and community . . . about Life and Death, as gloriously rich and funny as it inevitably turned out to be achingly sad.

All sorts of circumstances put us in the right place at the right time that July day, as if we'd been destined to be there, random circumstances that had all lined up just so.

Late that afternoon, I received an email from Carol Fertig telling me that Stephen had been in touch.

"I believe he told you a bit about my 'situation' and my beloved dog/child Harry. . . . Nothing would make me happier than knowing he would have a loving home to go to."

We agreed to meet the following Saturday.

Two:
INTELLIGENCE GATHERING

Suddenly, I was nervous. What was I getting myself into? Why was this beginning to remind me of online dating for dogs? Or two overly protective mothers trying to arrange a marriage?

A lot of emails went back and forth.

I sent a reply to Carol. I asked her to tell me about Harry, how old he was, whether he had health issues, if he got along with other dogs. She sent me this email the next morning:

From: Carol Fertig
To: Martha Teichner

M — So since last night I have been trying to figure out how I could succinctly describe Harry to you . . . an impossible task.

27

So, I thought I might as well get the "CONS" out of the way:

1. He takes meds; puppy Zoloft (he was a problem child apparently too much testosterone, he has now mellowed and is a big wooz) and Phenobarbital. He has taken these for years and have totally helped his "issues"-like going ballistic over skate boards and rolling suitcases. He takes Rymadyl for arthritis and Tynell (I think that's the name) for colitis. Dr. Farber is always impressed with his blood work and what good shape he is in.

2. I have trained Harry very well, he is a great listener but he does have a problem with large dogs. I have adjusted my own "radar" to keep an eye on this but I do have to be watching. Again, he is great with smaller dogs, always wagging his tail and wanting to engage-he especially loves those Frenchies.

3. I don't know if you have occasion to have a hose in your life, but if you do you can be sure he will destroy it as an act of protection of you. He also does this on the street

if he sees someone using one in the street.

4. He has a sensitive stomach so eats Dr. Hills special food. I order from Chewy.com every few weeks. All this to say he is on some level a money pit.

EXCENTRICITIES

When he was about 4 months old Harry discovered a metal bowl at the dog park. It has been in his life ever since. He is incredibly smart and after a time he figured out he could put a tennis ball (or 2) in the bowl and flip it out and catch it. He does this for hours and will entertain (or not) guests for hours with this "trick." I am going to send you videos of Harry with his bowl under separate cover.

PROS

1. He is at heart a big wooz, a love bug, a big baby.
2. He is so great with kids. The kids in my building adore him, they sit on him, stroke him, kiss him etc.
3. He is outgoing to friends (am sure your BT's the same, they are indeed

clowns).

4. He is so smart. He will figure out ways to let you know exactly how he feels (if I try to get him to do a second poop on the street and he doesn't want to he will just lay down in the street and not move until I finally give in and take him home).
5. Like all BTs he is relentless, notice how I put this under pros, it is one of the things I love about the breed. Having said this, he can tell by your tone what he should and should not do and will abide by your wishes.
6. He has a gentle bite.

Again, I am going to send you a number of short videos so you can see some of this for yourself.

I hope this is helpful.

Also, I am going to call Dr. Farber tomorrow to get his take on all this.

Again, looking forward.

Xc and H

A weird coincidence on top of a weird chance encounter . . . Carol and I took our dogs to the same vet, Dr. Michael Farber. I asked her to give him permission to talk to me about Harry. I said I would allow her to discuss Minnie and me with him. A breach of doctor/patient confidentiality in the name of matchmaking . . . and to calm what I realized was our mutual uneasiness.

A money pit? An animal who was obsessive-compulsive, had arthritis and chronic colitis, and attacked bigger dogs? Oh, dear. Good with kids though. I don't have any kids. Who in their right mind would look at Harry's list of pros and cons and think he'd be a good candidate for adoption?

Only a bull terrier lover.

On Sunday, Carol sent me a cell phone video of Harry putting multiple tennis balls into a metal bowl and waving it around, another of him attacking a hose on somebody's balcony, and a third of an unseen person (Carol) flinging his metal bowl like a Frisbee, the bowl clanging as it hits concrete, and Harry racing after it. I could see that he was mostly black and white. I sent her photos of a sleeping Minnie, white on white in my bathtub, where she likes to go when it's hot.

Carol replied:

31

OMG, those chunky little legs!!!! That Minnie!

Have put a call in to Dr. FARBER, will respond more fully once I have spoken with him.

Xc and H

On Monday, Dr. Farber reassured Carol that I am competent at dog care and would be a good dog stepmother for Harry. He admitted to me he'd advised Carol she had to come to terms with the likelihood she would have to have Harry put down, that it would be impossible to "rehome" him. Who would want an eleven-and-a-half-year-old dog with all those issues?

So, I thought, not only had Carol been told she had terminal cancer; if that wasn't nightmare enough, now she had to face the probability that the dog she loved more than anything would have to die, too, just because she was dying. What a horrible, double calamity. Dr. Farber didn't try to talk me into taking Harry. He did say Harry was sweet, his issues manageable, and that if we were careful about how we introduced Minnie and Harry, they would probably get along. He suggested short meetings, then longer visits, working up to sleepovers.

That night I dreamed Goose was alive. We were sitting in the back of a car. I was holding him. He was young, healthy, warm, his snuffly, sturdy, gentle self. When I woke up, and it wasn't true, I was desolate. I tried to wish the dream back, but it wouldn't come.

Carol and I decided to introduce the dogs the following Saturday.

In the meantime, I googled her. A bonanza. The first item to come up was from a website called New York Social Diary, dated January 2013, a long interview with all kinds of pictures. There was Carol sitting on a sofa with Harry draped across her lap. Harry with his metal bowl and tennis balls. Her Maine coon cat, Bruno. (A cat, too? Hmmm.) Objects Carol had designed. Objects Carol had collected. Her eclectic, stylish apartment. In her snug study, painted in a color called tangerine, a whole wall with photos and clippings pinned to it, pictures of fashionable people and clothing and furniture, castles, flowers, a Roman bust. *Vogue* magazine legend Diana Vreeland very much in evidence. Here and there snapshots of Carol dressed and made up to look like Vreeland, in Vreeland-like poses. The wall reminded me of storyboards I'd seen clothing designers use to inspire a look or a season, but covered with much, much more of everything, a thick clutter of ideas, overlapping like shingles on a roof. In the photographs, I saw shelves jam-packed with books surrounding an artfully arranged stack of a dozen or so orange Hermès boxes.

I clicked again and up came an article from 2012 in *Elle Decor* magazine about her apartment, a rental in what used to be the headquarters of JPMorgan, across the street from the New York Stock Exchange. Wow . . . no internationally known decorating magazine would do a story on my apartment. I scrolled down and found a page with a red logo at the top that said THE MET and then, under the heading "All Collection Records," a picture of a coat made out of pieced-together panels of rust and black wool. Date: early 1980s. Designer: Carol Fertig. Carol had a garment in the collection of the Metropolitan Museum of Art. Another wow.

I learned from my search that she'd designed clothing but also lots of other things: furniture, home accessories, even jewelry. She'd done brand strategy for a who's who in the fashion world, a bunch of those glamorous names whose ads for clothes and fragrances you have to page through before getting to the table of contents in magazines such as *Vogue* or *Vanity Fair.* In one interview, she admitted to being "addicted to television." In the mid-1980s, she was one of the founders of a magazine called *New York Woman.*

Peering at the pictures of Carol with her short, curly gray hair, in her big, owly glasses, I realized that I'd met her, long ago, sometime in the mid-to-late 1990s. Then, she had a different bull terrier, an all-white one. I was walking up Tenth Avenue one hot summer Sunday and came upon them at a restaurant with outdoor tables. I would tend to remember anyone with a bull terrier, but these two were singular. Carol was an imposing figure sitting there. She wore an extravagant, floppy-brimmed straw sun hat and giant dark glasses. The hazy snapshot in the back of my mind was of someone who looked slightly eccentric, flamboyant, wearing a dress that was ample and unconventional in some way. I explained to her that I, too, had a bull terrier, who was at home. His name was Piggy. She introduced the barrel-chested dog at her feet as Violet. Violet is not a name anyone would ever forget when attached to a bull terrier.

Bull terriers are odd dogs. With their egg-shaped heads, slitty eyes, and pointy ears, they're funny looking. Think Spuds Mac-Kenzie or the Target dog. BTs are opinionated, exuberant, stubborn, extremely silly, and loving, but at times too smart for their own good. What does that say about bull terrier owners? Every BT person I've ever met admits liking that these animals are subversive by nature. So right away, I figured that I understood something about Carol and that we'd get along.

I felt a little sneaky looking her up on the internet, but not that sneaky. Just about every time now I do an interview, the interview subject arrives with the printed-out results of a Google search and knows as much about me as I do. I'm sure Carol looked me up, too. She would have found out that I started at CBS News in 1977, that I've reported from all over the world: Latin America, Europe, the Middle East, and southern Africa. For more than a dozen years I was sent practically everywhere there was a war. She might have turned up a black-and-white photograph of me in a helmet sitting cross-legged in the Saudi desert during the Persian Gulf War in 1991, a tank shadowy behind me as I write in a reporter's notebook, or another, taken in 1988 on my fortieth birthday. I'm facing a cameraman about to do an on-camera. We're surrounded by what look like walking skeletons, victims of a civil war in Mozambique that lasted more than twenty years. They'd silently appeared out of the bush, most of them naked, at a camp where the charity CARE was offering them food. I remember interviewing a woman that day who was so emaciated that I could see her pulse through her chest, her heart beating just under her skin. I've been at *CBS Sunday Morning* since the end of 1993. It's been much safer.

If Carol had googled "Martha Teichner bull terriers," she would have seen a picture of me with Minnie and Goose, our heads together, all of us smiling.

As Saturday approached, I realized how much I wanted it to work out between Harry and Minnie. There were good arguments, a lot of them, against taking Harry, even if the two dogs got along. But I heard myself trying to rationalize away his negatives, trying to discount the fact that I would have Harry for the sad years of his life, the even more expensive years. I would be the one, not Carol, who would have to make the decision someday to put him to sleep. I was sure I would love him enough to be torn to pieces . . . again, when I had to hold him in my arms as he died, just as I was shattered when that moment came for Goose. I tried to be realistic, to put the brakes on my excitement, but I couldn't.

Minnie, I knew, wouldn't accept a younger dog. She doesn't like puppies, so the right companion for her had to be older, a dog who, almost certainly, would have issues, just as Harry did.

And there was another reason I was fighting my better judgment. My mother's dog, Winkie.

He was a Cairn Terrier, gray, like Toto in *The Wizard of Oz,* the last in a succession of Cairns my mother had over decades. When she retired to a house I'd bought her near Charleston, South Carolina, Winkie developed allergies so severe, his sides had nothing but patchy wisps of hair, more scabby skin than fur. He was only allowed outside on a fenced wooden deck that was always swept clean, so he wouldn't come in contact with grass or pine straw, which would make his allergies worse. Walks were forbidden. Nothing helped, not his weekly medicated baths, not the prednisone, which made him incontinent.

Winkie was timid. He trusted my mother but practically no one else. Even when he was a puppy, it took coaxing before he allowed me to pet him or play with him. He liked it when I put him in a shoulder bag and carried him around under my arm. He felt secure and would lick my face.

My mother lived a solitary life. She and Winkie had each other. It was enough, until my mother was diagnosed with colon cancer in 1990. I was living in London. I flew to Charleston and stayed with her for her surgery and as long as I could afterward. I was back for her second surgery a year later, when the colon cancer had spread to her liver, and for almost all the other times she was in the hospital. I was there, taking care of Winkie, and then I wasn't. An aunt also came and went, but too many times Winkie was alone in the house with a couple of lights left on for hours and hours and sometimes all night. When the person paid to come in and care for him arrived to feed him or let him out, he would hide under my mother's bed.

Her cancer was terminal, and she knew it. She said she wanted Winkie put down after her death, his ashes buried with hers. In addition to his skin problems, he was ten and had cataracts. He was another dog with "issues." No one wanted him either. I couldn't take him. I already had a dog, and I wasn't sure Winkie, with so many health concerns, would even survive the mandatory six-month quarantine England required then before admitting pets.

I was with my mother when she died and then stayed on in South Carolina for a few weeks to clear up her affairs. Winkie and I spent time together. Having him near me was a comfort. I think he was glad to have company. I cuddled him and tried to make him feel loved. I made calls, lots of them, trying, hoping, somehow to find a home for him, but my mother had been right. No one wanted him. I put off following her wishes until I couldn't anymore. I had to go back to work, back to London. Time was up.

On the morning of the appointment with the vet, I fed Winkie a whole meal of ground sirloin and took him to the beach to play, something he hadn't been allowed to do for years because of his allergies. We spent hours there. I didn't want to leave because I knew what was next. I stood over him sobbing, my eyes blurred as I watched him. Was I crying for him, for my mother, or for myself? He poked his little nose in the sand and then sneezed. He ran and sniffed and peed and seemed surprised to find out that the ocean was wet and was delighted to be outside and free.

And then I had him killed. The vet wouldn't let me hold him. She said, "No, I'm taking him to the back." I begged, but she was firm. I stood at the receptionist's desk waiting, imagining, knowing exactly what was happening behind the door that was closed to me. Maybe five minutes later, the receptionist's phone rang. She answered it, listened, then looked up at me. "It's done," she said. I paid and left. How could it be that ending his life would appear as an entry on my credit card statement?

My next stop was a travel agency, to arrange taking my mother's ashes and Winkie's to northern Michigan, to be buried next to my father, not far from where I'd lived as a child. When the travel agent greeted me, I tried to speak but couldn't. My jaws hurt, I'd been clenching them so hard.

Nearly thirty years later, I still cry when I think about what I did to that poor, sad little dog. I know that's why I hoped with all my heart that Minnie and Harry would get along, no matter what happened then.

I asked myself whether I should tell Carol about Winkie when she came over with Harry and then decided . . . no, too soon. It might upset her, or she might assume I would automatically take Harry out of guilt.

As the day of the meeting approached, I found myself wondering how time seemed to Carol. Her days had become a measurable countdown to the end. When I saw her, would she look and act like a dying woman?

And then it was Saturday . . . Saturday, July 30, 2016, the big day. I took Minnie to the farmers market as usual, feeling giddy, excited. I came home to emails from Carol, logistics mainly. One o'clock at my front door. Stephen set to arrive at her building at 12:30 P.M. The drive shouldn't take long, but Carol pointed out that Stephen was notorious for being late. Did she feel giddy and excited, too? When you know you'll be dead in a few months, is it possible to get excited about anything? I found out the answer was yes.

About noon, I emailed Carol that I'd given Minnie a bath so she would be shiny and white, alluring for her "blind date." Carol replied that she offered to put some Eau Sauvage behind Harry's ears, but he'd refused. Not only excited, I thought, but capable of being silly. We were two hopeless romantics, matchmaking.

THREE:
HARRY MEETS MINNIE

One o'clock came and went. No Carol. No Harry. No Stephen. I fussed. I petted Minnie. I looked out my front windows. I checked my cell phone. I paced. I tried to read the newspaper. Two o'clock came and went. My fussing notched up. Finally, I got a text from Carol. Stephen was late. I heard from her again. Horrific traffic on the West Side Highway. There are other routes, but normally, as long as it's not rush hour, this expressway along the Hudson River was the quickest, twenty minutes between Carol's place and mine, no more. At two-thirty, she texted to say they were still on the West Side Highway. They were stuck. No way to exit. I began pacing and fussing all over again. Where were they? Why was I so anxious?

Finally, just before three, Carol phoned to tell me they were on my block, looking for a parking space. I grabbed my keys, rushed outside, and stood on the top step looking around. Nothing. I kept looking. Now what? Maybe five minutes later, I saw a woman a few buildings along, squeezing her way between parked cars onto the sidewalk. She was looking down. She stopped and started, tugging at something, coaxing, pleading with whatever it was in a high voice. A large black-and-white bull terrier appeared, stepping out from the flowers around one of the trees that line the street, a little garden fenced to keep dogs away. He took his time to pee and sniff as the two of them made their way slowly in my direction. Carol and Harry had arrived. I saw Stephen in the distance standing by the open tailgate of an old Land Rover staring after them.

I knew what Carol looked like from my online search, but she was much taller than I realized, six feet or very close to it, full-figured but not fat. She was wearing huge black glasses, even owlier than the ones in the pictures I'd seen, and a loose gray dress with sleeves just covering her shoulders, a thin white T-shirt underneath. I wondered whether it was one of her own designs. Something about her demanded attention, to how she looked, to what she had on. I, on the other hand, was wearing my customary black leggings and a black jacket with a bandanna at the neck. Not exactly the ideal outfit for someone with a white dog.

Carol's gray ringlets circled her head like a cap, springy in the summer humidity. She had a long neck, and for some reason the way she carried herself — head held high, chin and jaw erect — reminded me of the famous bust of Nefertiti in Berlin's Egyptian Museum. No one would ever have called Carol pretty. She was arresting, with her nearly nonexistent eyebrows carefully penciled in, with her very red lipstick, her long face, long nose.

Her voice was the surprise. It was high and wistful, vulnerable as she introduced herself. Such a soft, almost girlish sound coming from someone so imposing; not what I expected. When I'd heard her trying to get Harry out of the flowers, I assumed she was talking dog baby-talk to him, but I was wrong.

Harry was handsome, much taller than Minnie, lean. He had a big white splotch on his back. I can't decide whether it looked like a boomerang or Harry Potter's lightning scar. Maybe that's why his name was Harry. Bull terriers are supposed to have large, egg-shaped heads. Harry's was perfect, and he had lovely, soulful eyes, but as he reached my front stoop, I saw he was limping, favoring his right front foot. What was that about? And there was the matter of his three collars. Three. One was a serious black-leather, punk number at least two inches wide, studded with inch-square brass pyramids. Another was a necklace of linked steel prongs intended to dig into his neck whenever he tried to pull. Yikes. The third was the kind of braided cord dog handlers use in the show ring, also black. Did he belong to a gang? Was this dog dangerous? He reminded me of the front door of a New York City apartment with three hulking dead bolts to keep intruders out.

By this time, Stephen had caught up and said hello. He and Carol and Harry settled themselves on the stoop outside the brownstone where my apartment is, a brownstone being a row house faced with soft brown stone or stucco. A stoop, for anyone who doesn't live in New York City, is the staircase leading to the front door. New Yorkers hang out on their stoops or on other people's, eat on their stoops, people watch on their stoops. On this particular Saturday, my stoop was meant to be neutral territory; in theory, a safe place to introduce the two dogs.

Looking at Harry, I wondered whether it *was* safe to bring Minnie out to meet him. What had I gotten myself into?

46

Minnie had no intention of cooperating as I hooked on her leash. When bull terriers don't want to move, so help me, they lower their center of gravity and make themselves heavier. Wrangling her out my front door and through the lobby was an ordeal. Minnie didn't seem particularly eager to meet anyone. Outside, she took one look at Harry, turned around, and plopped down with her backside to his face. Very rude. I sat on the top step. Harry ignored Minnie's slight and stuck his nose in my pocket, where the treats were.

Stephen, by his own admission, talks a lot, which was good on this occasion, since none of us was too sure how to handle the meeting. Was it an interview? A social occasion? A dog date? At first, we were all a little tense, except for Harry and Minnie.

Harry, Carol informed me, was from Bedlam bull terriers, a famous line of champions. His breeder had won the Bull Terrier Club of America's Silverwood Competition, the most important event for the breed in the United States, where the top dog each year is judged the best-bred bull terrier in the country. Harry came from the last litter of Bedlam puppies before the breeder retired. Carol couldn't remember his formal, registered name and had lost his pedigree papers.

I told her what I repeat to anyone who asks, that although Minnie was from a dog pound, her bloodlines unknown, she was convinced she was a glamorous movie star or maybe a princess.

Every bull terrier owner has a "how I fell in love with bull terriers in the first place" story, since most people look at a BT and wonder why on earth anyone would choose such an animal. I've been told they look prehistoric. Four different times, I've been asked whether my dog was an anteater.

While I was based in South Africa, I did a story on a star rugby-player-turned-winemaker who had a red bull terrier. The dog followed me around the winery. When I sat down, he sat down, too, on my feet. My hands just naturally found his soft ears. When I stood up, he leaned against my leg. I liked his sturdy body. I'd been wanting a dog. This was the kind of dog I had to have. His name was Petrus. I assumed he was named for Château Pétrus, one of the most expensive and sought-after red wines in the world, but, no, the dog's name was not the winemaker's in-joke. The name was from the Afrikaans word for "rock" or "hard place." How odd, I thought at the time. Only later, when I had a rock-hard-headed, stubborn bull terrier of my own, did I understand.

Carol's story: She sees a BT and thinks it's so extraordinary looking, just from a design perspective, she has to have one. She does some research and discovers that the person most closely associated with bull terriers in the United States is a breeder and show judge named Mary Remer. Carol makes an appointment and goes to see her at her home in Pennsylvania, along suburban Philadelphia's elite suburban rail corridor known as the Main Line. Carol finds herself outside elaborate wrought-iron gates, which open slowly and majestically to a tree-lined drive. The reveal at the end: Ardrossan, the grand fifty-room mansion that was once home to socialite Hope Montgomery Scott, the inspiration for Katharine Hepburn's character in the play and Academy Award–winning film *The Philadelphia Story*. Carol described walking into a house straight out of the English countryside, baronial, filled with antiques and paintings and beautiful woodwork. Mary Remer is Hope Montgomery Scott's granddaughter and lives in the house with a few of her relatives and many bull terriers. In fact, Carol said, bull terriers were everywhere. In a dining room that suggested Downton Abbey, dog beds and crates were lined up side by side against the walls, like extra chairs. Violet, Carol's first bull terrier, was the result of her visit. Carol's story was much better than mine.

I told her I'd met her before, for a few minutes, with Violet at the outdoor restaurant all those years ago. Then she startled me with a revelation of her own, about another curious coincidence, another uncanny bit of serendipity connected with this adventure. Carol was at the vet's office once with Harry when someone was picking up one of my dogs. Probably Goose, I thought. She heard the vet tech call out my name, looked up, and saw a BT. "Martha Teichner has a bull terrier," Carol noted to herself. "Huh, what do you know?" She was aware of who I was because she was a fan of *CBS Sunday Morning*. "When I was diagnosed," she went on, "when my situation became clear, one of the first things I thought, fantasized really, was 'Wouldn't it be great if Martha Teichner took Harry?' I couldn't believe it when Stephen called and said that you'd lost Goose and were looking for an older male to keep Minnie company."

I don't use the word *freaky* often, but this *was* freaky.

Carol explained her Sunday ritual. She

50

and Harry slept in. She recorded *CBS Sunday Morning.* Late in the day, she watched the show while she assembled Harry's Tylan capsules. What? One of his "issues" was chronic colitis. At breakfast and dinner, he had to take Tylan, a medication I'd never heard of. At the local compounding pharmacy for animals, Tylan capsules are expensive, Carol told me, so she ordered a capsule-making kit online and bought jars of powdered Tylan from our mutual vet. While watching *Sunday Morning* on Sunday afternoon, while watching *me,* she pressed empty capsule shells into holes in two plastic frames, poured in the yellow Tylan powder, then pressed the two frames together. Presto, capsules that pop out onto a plate perfectly formed. Not so hard.

Carol took a plastic bag out of her handbag and pulled out wedges of something orangey-colored, shriveled up, and tinged with black. I noticed the slight tremor in her fingers. "Sweet potato treats. High fiber, good for colitis. I bake them. If you decide to take Harry, I'll show you how," she said, then realized she might be scaring me off. She sounded a little desperate, a little sad. "I hope you'll think about taking him anyway. He's very sweet."

I admired Harry's brass-studded collar.

Carol admired Minnie's "jewels."

"I want to keep him till the very end," Carol said abruptly.

When would that be? Dr. Farber said she'd been told six months to a year. Carol had spoken only of her "situation." She was diagnosed in May. We were at the end of July. Somehow I'd thought that if I agreed to take Harry, it would happen right away. But for Carol, having Harry with her was about hanging on to Life itself. So I said nothing. What was there to say? If I were the one dying, I wouldn't want to let go, not until I had no choice. Anyway, it was far from clear that I'd take Harry. We didn't know yet whether the two dogs would even get along.

"By the way, who takes care of Minnie when you travel?" Carol asked. I explained that I had a "dog au pair," someone who lives in and does dog care when I need it in exchange for room and board. "Of course you do," she replied, and laughed. I saw a shiny, clear plastic patch stuck to the back of her left forearm and thought . . . Ah, for pain.

Suddenly, Minnie got up and turned around, startling Harry. They settled back down, but now Minnie was side by side with Harry. Carol and Stephen and I shifted a

52

little on the hard steps. We all laughed and began to talk politics, all three of us news junkies. It was an election-year summer. The Republican National Convention had just taken place. Donald Trump had been nominated by the Republican Party to run for president against Hillary Clinton. Lots to talk about and much more fun than talking about death. We relaxed.

It started to rain. Carol and Stephen decided it was time to leave. Before they left, Carol took a cell phone picture of me with Harry and Minnie. Later, it occurred to me that, instead, we should have gotten Stephen to take a picture of both Carol and me with the dogs.

The next day, Harry sent Minnie an email (with Carol's help) saying how much he liked her, although he wasn't sure she liked him. He hoped she would invite him back. A courtship of sorts was underway.

FOUR:
ANOTHER, VERY DIFFERENT
CHANCE ENCOUNTER

The story I'm going to tell you now has nothing whatsoever to do with Harry and Minnie, *except* that it's about another chance encounter that changed my life.

In 2005, right after New Year's, while I was in South Carolina for the holidays, I was introduced to Jeannie and Gordon Hillock, who own a home near Traverse City, Michigan, where I was born. We became friends. They invited me to visit them in Michigan that summer, along with Frank Manganello, the mutual friend who'd introduced us. I wonder now, what if I hadn't met them just when I did? What if I hadn't taken them up on their invitation?

Hold the back of your left hand in front of your face, little finger spread to the left, thumb spread to the right, three middle fingers together. You know real Michiganders by this gesture, the way you know Trekkies by theirs. Ask Michiganders where they're from, and they'll thrust out their left hands and point at the freckle or the vein or the fingernail that coincides with their hometown on flesh-and-blood maps of Michigan they can slip out of their pockets anytime. Traverse City is at the bottom of the *V* between the ring finger and the pinkie. The space in between, the spread, is Grand Traverse Bay, which opens out into Lake Michigan.

Downtown Traverse City isn't any bigger than it was when I was a child, but there are trendy restaurants on Front Street now. A gathering of food trucks is called the Little Fleet. The social gadfly and filmmaker Michael Moore has moved to Traverse City, restored the old State Theatre, and started a wildly popular film festival. Development is rippling outward, creating small-time sprawl, but driving into town around the curve of the lake is still thrilling and beautiful. You can still watch storm clouds form and take over the sky in minutes, turning the bay from brilliant blue to black, from gentle to mean. Sometimes, on clear nights, you can look out over the lake and see the northern lights paint the sky with curtains and swirls of eerie color, purple and green and red, bright enough so they reflect in the water. Traverse City calls itself the Cherry

Capital of the World because the area produces more sour cherries, pie cherries, than anywhere else, but it's known for its wineries as well. It's the center of the region's tourist universe.

Stick out your left hand again. See Traverse City? Starting there, trace around your little finger, the whole thing. That's Leelanau County, pronounced LEE-luh-gnaw, maybe even more beautiful, with its astonishing one hundred miles of Lake Michigan shoreline. If you were driving that route, more or less at the point where your little finger meets the rest of your hand, you'd come to the Sleeping Bear Dunes, sand dunes 450 feet high and spectacular, now part of a national park, the Sleeping Bear Dunes National Lakeshore. Until you see them, you have no concept of how big they are, these colossal white sand cliffs. From the top of the dunes, Lake Michigan, far below, spreads out like a flat blue floor all the way to the horizon.

Leelanau County has dozens of much smaller lakes, too. They play hide-and-seek with you as you drive the narrow roads. They twinkle from behind trees and flirt, teasing you with a glimpse of beach, like a flutter of petticoat, before disappearing when a hill gets in the way or an orchard or a farm. After World War II, my parents bought forty acres of woods and a boarded-up old house on one of them, Lime Lake, a half-hour drive northwest of Traverse City. They fixed up the house, called it Deer Trail Cottage, and loved it desperately. All their dreams found a home there. Great, ancient maples and beeches stood guard outside our doors and held off the forest lurking where the grass ended.

From the time I was old enough to feel anything, what I felt was the wildness of where I lived. I am an only child, to this day a solitary person, comfortable with being alone. I had no playmates until I went to school, except when my cousins visited in the summer. So I noticed my surroundings, which had stories to tell.

We had no close neighbors. The nearest house was a quarter of a mile or so away, but no one lived there. It was quiet enough to hear cars a long way off, to know by the sound when they rounded certain curves, went up and then down hills, making their way along the gravel road, slowly getting louder as they came closer, finally reaching our house in a cloud of dust. The bark of a dog echoed all the way across the lake. We often saw deer and foxes, sometimes bears and even wolves. At night we heard whip-poor-wills and owls and loons, their calls lonely and pure, coming from someplace deep in the velvety blackness beyond the insect chorus. I watched fireflies out my bedroom window. Wild blackberries grew in a tangle at the edge of our driveway.

My favorite thing in the world was to go for a walk in the woods behind our house with my father. In the spring it was carpeted with wildflowers: Dutchman's-breeches and jack-in-the-pulpit and glorious, white trillium. Morel mushrooms pushed up through generations of dead leaves. Shelves of strange fungus grew on fallen trees and patches of moss shaped like imaginary countries. As we walked, my father would sing German songs to me, the songs of his childhood in Bavaria before World War I.

The path to the lake was different. My parents held my hand as we crossed the road and descended into what we called "the swamp," a moist, dense cedar forest that was dark and fragrant, a little frightening. We balanced on planks and tippy logs at spots where streams bubbled up along the way. Our dogs loved rolling in the muck whenever it was particularly wet.

Trees grew all the way to the water's edge. The lake was warm as bathwater, hot almost, where it was shallow, its sandy bottom covered with thousands and thousands of smooth, slimy boards, layered on one another, shoved into the water when a sawmill once located nearby burned down in 1897, more than half a century before I was born. Every summer my father hired a man with a bulldozer, who came and piled boards into a huge heap. When they dried, and the snapping turtles had all run off, we would build a bonfire that would burn itself down to the water. Every spring, there were more boards. Go there now. You'll see them.

Once, shortly before she died, I asked my mother if she remembered anything hopelessly romantic, the most romantic thing she and my father used to do together. In all my memories of them together, they were young and strong and wonderful to watch. She sat for a long time without responding, then said quietly, simply, "In the summer, when the moon was full, sometimes at night, we would go down to Lime Lake. We would push out the raft and swim in the moonlight." We had a housekeeper, so it wasn't as if they were leaving their sleeping child alone in the house.

In my mind I could see them slip out, hear the sound of their breathing, of their footsteps as they descended the path to the lake. I imagined the water, calm and silvery in the night stillness, rippling softly, lapping their bodies as they moved through it, bathed in moonlight, the sky alive with stars, the magic of being there alone filling their hearts. This had been my mother's secret, a small, special treasure she had stored away for decades, so precious she only allowed me a glimpse of it as she was dying. When I wrote about it, after all I'm about to tell you had taken place, I said, "My mother's gift to me of a silver, moonlit memory, I pass on now. . . ." I say it again, here.

I believe that in the country, where the earth hasn't been paved over, a place, a piece of land, can become part of us. We eat what its soil has produced. We drink water that has passed through it. We feel it inside ourselves as surely as if it were in our DNA.

My mother and I never, ever, truly recovered from the loss of our home, when it was sold, and we moved to another part of the state the year after my father died. I was ten. Just as we held it in our very chemistry, it held us. The ghosts of our memories were still there among the trees, the sound of my father's laugh in the wind through their branches. For more than thirty years, we stayed away.

In 1992, I came back with my mother's

ashes and Winkie's, to bury them next to my father in a cemetery at the edge of another of Leelanau County's lakes, under a towering pine tree that was a sapling in 1957, when I'd seen it last.

I drove past our house, someone else's for longer than it had belonged to us. It was a different color, not white with green shutters anymore. My mother's bright flower gardens and my swing and the sign that said DEER TRAIL COTTAGE were gone. Our low cedar hedge had grown into a line of tall trees shielding the house from the road, which had been paved. I kept driving. A little farther along, the old Ludwig house was leaning to the right, about to fall in. I stopped. By some strange coincidence . . . or not . . . I had just received an order from the county to demolish it.

When I was maybe four or five, my grandmother, my mother's mother, bought the twenty acres next to our forty, known to everyone for miles around as "the Ludwig place." The house was empty, the Ludwigs long gone. I don't remember it having indoor plumbing. It smelled musty, but to me and to my cousins it was fascinating and mysterious because it contained a post office dating back to the 1890s, the old sawmill days, not much more than an attached shed, but still there in the 1950s. In the alphabetized mail slots, we found letters, their scrawly, handwritten addresses faded, to and from real people, surely dead by then. There was something forbidden about them, as if opening the dusty envelopes would have allowed evil spirits to escape. We did open some and lived.

My grandmother had planned to remodel the house and move there from Chicago. She died before it could happen. At first, all of her children paid the taxes and argued about what to do with the property. Then one by one they stopped, until finally, after maybe thirty years, my mother was the only one who paid anything. The property ended up hers, and when she died, mine. By then, I was paying the taxes. I suppose the timing, the fact that I had notified the county of my mother's death, explained how it happened that just at that moment I was informed that the house was a hazard. The notice ordered me not only to knock it down but also to fill in the well, meaning that legally the property would be considered undeveloped, as if no one had ever lived there. When the job was done, I received photographs of a mound of earth with a polite ring of trees around it, like mourners at a new grave.

My next visit to the area was four years later, in 1996. By then I'd moved back to the United States from London to work at *CBS Sunday Morning*. The private school where my father taught for many years had invited me to speak. The organizers of the event asked if there was anything special I'd like to do. I said yes, I'd like to be driven around Lime Lake. As we passed the old Ludwig place, my twenty acres, I heard the growls of earthmoving equipment. Just beyond my property line I saw acres and acres of torn-up land. "What is *this*?" I asked in shock. The woman driving me answered, "They're building a golf course."

As beautiful as some golf courses are, the chemicals used to keep them that way can harm the soil and water nearby and even the wildlife. What would become of Lime Lake? What would happen to the woods? Would there be pressure on landowners to sell to developers? Development begets development, I've found. Just outside the national park, this little lakeside seemed to have CONDO written all over it. So much for wild. I asked whether some nature organization was trying to protect land in Leelanau County. Yes, I was told, the Leelanau Conservancy. That was on a Saturday.

On Monday, I called and gave my twenty

acres to the Leelanau Conservancy. It became the Teichner Preserve. I was asked to write something for the conservancy's newsletter. I said I hoped my gift would inspire other property owners to protect land around Lime Lake, but no one did, not then.

Twenty years had passed when I accepted my new friends' invitation to visit them in northern Michigan. I hadn't been back in all that time. I was excited to be there. Jeannie and Gordon Hillock have what I consider the perfect summer home on a little string of lakes east of Traverse City and are wonderful hosts. They were planning a party to celebrate Gordon's sixtieth birthday, but Jeannie and Frank Manganello, the mutual friend who'd introduced us, suggested we make time to drive the fifty miles or so to Lime Lake so they could see the Teichner Preserve and where I lived as a child.

Here's where what seemed like random, unrelated events turned out to be anything but. If we had done just one thing differently, none of what happened would have taken place. People can say what they like about Fate, deny it exists, but how I've managed to be in the right place at the right time more than once amazes me.

We were originally going to make our trip to Lime Lake on Monday, but then changed our minds and decided to go on Sunday morning instead. What if we hadn't? There are a lot of what-ifs about this story. Jeannie said, "Oh, let's stop in Cedar and go to Pleva's." The village of Cedar, population slightly over ninety, was on our way. My mother started shopping at Pleva's in the late 1940s, long before it became famous locally for its sausage made with cherries. In cherry country, you can buy cherry anything. When we got to Cedar, we discovered Pleva's didn't open until eleven o'clock. We sat in the car watching the door as if we were on a stake-out. When we saw the CLOSED sign being flipped over, we made for the door and were the first customers inside. We sampled sausage and made our choices and discussed the framed newspaper clipping on the wall about the Pleva girl who had been Traverse City's National Cherry Queen in 1987. We decided to go to the general store, next door, because it had an extensive selection of Leelanau County and Traverse City area wines. We wanted to buy a case for the party. It's illegal in Leelanau County to buy alcohol before noon on Sundays, so we had to wait some more. I reminisced about the Cedar of my childhood with its one blinking yellow light; the little former bank building that the Casben family turned into a meat locker, where hunters paid to hang the carcasses of the deer they shot to age; the family restaurant friends of my parents owned in the building where the general store was — history that only mattered to me. Cedar hadn't changed much, except that it had gotten smaller. We chatted with the owner of the store, who knew which of the local wines were actually good, until finally, he looked at his watch and announced that it was noon. We paid and headed off toward Lime Lake.

As we neared the house, Jeannie asked, "Do you want to see if anyone's home?" I hemmed and hawed. Unless I'm working, I'm shy, not the sort of person who talks to strangers. "Well, it might be an intrusion. I don't know the people who live there. What do you think? Maybe we shouldn't. . . ." Jeannie ignored me and pulled into the driveway. I felt uncomfortable and nervous. A woman about my age with short blondish hair was sitting in a lawn chair next to the dining room door, speaking on a cell phone. As the three of us — Jeannie, Frank, and I — got out of the car, I saw the woman say something into her phone and put it down on the arm of the chair. She stood up, stared at us, stared at me for a couple of seconds, then threw her arms open wide and beamed. "You're Martha Teichner. I've been waiting all these years for you to come!" Later, Frank, an opera fan, said the scene reminded him of something from an opera.

The woman embraced me and said her name was Janna Blakely and that if we'd arrived any earlier, she and her husband, Eric, wouldn't have been home. We told her we'd thought about coming the next day but changed our minds. "Good thing you did. Tomorrow we won't be here. We'll be at work." The Blakelys invited us in.

Forty-seven years. I did the arithmetic in my head as I walked from room to room. It had been forty-seven years since I'd been in that house. The Blakelys had made changes, but my memory of how it felt to live in its space flooded back. I could almost see my father's morris chair in the den with its yellow leather cushions, where I sat on his lap. In the dark hall I could almost see what we called "the petting stool," where our German shepherd had been taught to park his front paws, so he wouldn't knock us over when he greeted us in the morning at the bottom of the stairs. My old bedroom was just as I remembered it, a tiny wedge of a thing, tucked under the slant of the roof, with that window all the way to the floor. I realized for the first time that nothing in the entire house was symmetrical, and I wondered, as I had a thousand times, about the mystery of the floorboards, maple in some rooms, pine or oak in others, wide in the den and the hall, narrow everywhere else. As we all sat in the living room, Janna Blakely asked me where my family had put our Christmas tree. I pointed to a space to the right of the fireplace. She laughed. "That's where we put ours." Then she asked the most important question: "Do you want to walk down to the lake?"

Instead of the dark and fragrant swamp I remembered, closing in on us as we made our way along the old muddy path down, down into its green thickness, there was a gravel road wider than a car. The huge old cedars, so many were gone, what was left of them broken and toppled over, dead, their roots exposed, like casualties of war abandoned on a battlefield. The route to the lake was bright and hot and dry. I know that a child's perception of a place is different from an adult's, but I couldn't have been that wrong. This place had been violated. It had lost its will to live.

The Blakelys told me they owned only the

house and one acre around it. Piece by piece, the land my family had owned was sold off by one owner after another. I said that for much of my life I'd dreamed of buying it all back, even the house if it was ever for sale. Eric Blakely told me that the previous summer, a good-size chunk *had* been on the market, maybe seventeen acres, he recalled, all the land between the house and the lake. Some kind of speculator owned it. "Is it still for sale?" I asked. "Could you please make quiet inquiries without mentioning my name?"

I felt light-headed, disoriented. Conversations buzzed around me like clouds of insects. The rest of my visit to Michigan was a haze. All I could think about was another what-if, what if I could actually buy those seventeen acres and give them to the Leelanau Conservancy, add on to the Teichner Preserve? I had no idea what it would cost or how I'd find the money, but if I could, I would.

A few days after I got back to New York, the Blakelys called, appalled by what the owner had told them. He'd been granted a permit to cut down trees and fill in the wetlands. He planned to build another road, like the one down to the lake, and at least one spec house. He had hired work crews.

They were coming in two weeks. *No. No.* A voice in my head shouted, "I have to stop him." I felt sick. Enough damage had been done.

I phoned the Leelanau Conservancy, asked for help, and waited.

We were up against that two-week deadline, caught in a relentless countdown. The more I learned, the more I worried. The owner had a bad reputation. He had built spec projects before on other lakes: houses, a kind of marina. From what people at the conservancy could find out, all tacky, insensitive to nature. When he applied for his permit to build on Lime Lake, neighbors who discovered what he wanted to do were alarmed. They held meetings, petitioned the state, did everything they could to protest a project they argued would cause irreparable harm to the watershed, to the ecology of the lake . . . and lost. The State of Michigan Department of Environmental Quality has to approve any request to fill in wetlands. The way it was explained to me, if the DEQ fails to act on an application in three months, it's automatically granted. That's apparently how the developer got permission. Property owners on Lime Lake were angry and suspicious. They had made enough noise that the bureaucrats couldn't have just forgotten.

Then, knowing none of this, I showed up on a Sunday morning, not a Monday, when the Blakelys happened to have just gotten home. Was it chance? Or was it my parents, heartsick, reaching out from somewhere beyond the grave, guiding me to where I needed to be? How to explain such things . . . ?

The Leelanau Conservancy tried to convince the owner that if he sold the land to me, he wouldn't have to borrow money and pay interest on it until the development was completed and sold. Who knew how long it would all take? By selling, he wouldn't have to do anything. He'd be cashing out and making a profit immediately. No risk involved. But would he agree?

"Probably not," I was told, "but we'll keep trying." Days went by; for me, terrible days. A woman who owned the seven acres of lakefront next to the Teichner Preserve called the conservancy with another proposal. "I don't think he'll say yes, but if you can pull this off, I'll give you my land."

Finally, the call came. The owner was willing to sell, but the price was four hundred thousand dollars, and he wanted a quick closing. What? The year before he'd been asking less than a hundred thousand. I

71

couldn't come up with that much money. "How much can you do?" the conservancy lawyer asked. "I could refinance my apartment in New York and pull out" — I went quiet as I tried to figure out what was possible — "maybe two hundred thousand dollars. That's a lot of money for me, but I think I can get that much." My stomach was churning. It would be so easy to turn my back. I thought, You're crazy. *Borrow* two hundred thousand dollars and give it away?

But if I didn't, what then? How could I live with myself? I was sure that somehow my parents would find a way to haunt me, curse me forever, strike me dead. No, I mean it. The Teichner Preserve was named not for me but for them. "I can do it, not in a week or two, though."

The director of the conservancy had a plan. "We have some money available from bequests. How about we buy the property, and then you pay us the two hundred thousand dollars when you get it?"

And that's what happened, all of it.

I tell this story of another chance encounter as a way of putting Harry and Minnie's story in context. I have no idea why such things happen to me, or to anyone. They just do.

FIVE:
SATURDAY, AUGUST 6

Visit number two, a week after visit number one, was less hectic and more fun. Stephen took another route. He was only a little bit late. Carol and I decided we could allow the dogs to meet inside my apartment. When I opened my front door, Minnie stood beside me, head up, trying to figure out what was going on. Harry pushed right past her and began exploring. He went straight to a big wicker basket, overflowing with dog toys, most of them Goose's. Minnie doesn't play with toys, but I couldn't bring myself to throw them away after Goose's death. Harry inspected the balls and ropes and stuffed animals on top, like a kid in an ice cream parlor checking out the flavors, helped himself, and pulled his choices down to the floor one after another.

Stephen burst in, an explosion of energy entering my apartment. Carol followed. She sat down at my dining table, opened her purse, and took out a plastic bag bulging with pieces of roast chicken, then, another one filled with cooked ground beef. "I want Minnie to associate Harry with good things," she told me. "That'll do it," I replied.

Next, she reached in and produced a wide, weathered red leather collar, trimmed with brass cutouts: a shepherd and his dog, three cows, two medallions. "Swiss," she said. "It belonged to Violet. Harry wanted Minnie to have it."

I laughed. "A family heirloom. He's trying to impress her. Thank you." Here we were acting out a fantasy courtship on behalf of our dogs, like little girls playing with their dolls. The romantic story we were inventing seemed very Jane Austen. Is Harry Mr. Darcy? I wondered. I've always dreamed about being wooed this way. If only. I put the collar on Minnie. It looked very fancy next to her jewels. I remembered the motto of a wonderful, over-the-top line of women's shoes I used to buy sometimes: Too Much Is Never Enough. That's Minnie.

Then I thought, Carol is starting to let go of her treasures. What an act of courage.

In my bedroom closet, among the folded turtlenecks and T-shirts and sweaters, I have a secret little shrine. On one shelf Piggy's tough-guy, spiked collar, punk, like Harry's, sits on top of the flimsy carton filled with his ashes, a tiny fake rose tucked under the plastic shrink-wrap half crushing the box. The crematorium should have done better. I've thought about getting Piggy a proper urn, but I never have. I bought the collar in an act of mortified contrition after Piggy dragged me into a pet shop and started devouring all the treats in the baskets lined up by the door and hanging on hooks just within grabbing range, low-hanging fruit put there intentionally, but theft nonetheless.

One shelf down, Goose's plain woven collar, faded green and frayed, with all his tags still attached, hangs over the edge of his urn, a better one, made out of wood. My dead dogs' collars are like my father's watch or the scarves my mother wore, things I can touch, things that make me remember, not worth anything to anyone else, but priceless to me. By giving Violet's collar to Minnie, Carol invested it with new meaning. Now it was my treasure, too. And when I said to her, "This must be very difficult for you," she answered. "It actually gives me pleasure." But that doesn't mean it wasn't hard.

I love portraits. My living room is filled with pictures of people I've never met: a little girl holding a bunch of flowers painted sometime around 1830 on a wooden board, a woman peering out a window at the sea wondering whether her fisherman husband was coming back, an Englishman dressed for a fox hunt in a red coat and riding hat, and some old oils I bought when I was sent to Moscow during the collapse of the Soviet Union, among my favorites. I also have a painting of Goose, a serious likeness, not intended to be cute. It hangs above where his crate used to be, next to Minnie's. I know, dog crates in the living room, an eyesore, but I don't care. Carol made her way around the room looking at the pictures and then peered out the back door at my balcony and garden, no doubt trying to imagine Harry there. She said nothing.

I sat in the middle of the couch, Minnie snuggled up against my left leg. As I watched Carol, trying to see my home through her eyes, Harry put his front paws up on my right side, begging for a boost. I scooped him up so I was sandwiched between the two of them. Suddenly, Minnie stiffened, a growl rumbling in her throat. She turned her head toward Harry as if she were about to lunge at him. I grabbed her collars and held her back, facing her with a ferocious stare. Carol and Stephen looked terrified. I petted Minnie and tried to reassure her, and eventually she relaxed. So did the rest of us. We dared to breathe. Harry seemed oblivious. After a few minutes, he jumped down and started exploring again, opening the door to Minnie's crate with his nose and poking his head inside.

Minnie's threatening little outburst had us worried that maybe the dogs might not get along. We went silent, aware of the implications, then tried to chat our way out of the tension we all felt. Stephen brought up politics. We eventually moved on to our dogs' habits, good and bad. I described how mine have all loved fruit. "We have our daily fruit ritual after our morning walk. We always start with a banana. Then we have an orange. We go through everything available: apples, pears, kiwis, whatever is in season. Goose liked strawberries. Minnie doesn't. Apricots, plums, pineapple, mangoes, raspberries, cantaloupe, peaches, nectarines. Cherries. I bite them in half and pick the pit out for them. Minnie doesn't like blackberries. We always end with dates. Again, I take the half with the pit. When Goose or Piggy had their dates, they'd just walk out of the kitchen. Now Minnie gets up on my bed, and I bring her fruit to her. She likes room service." I heard myself and thought, Carol must think I'm nuts.

She laughed. "I've never really given Harry fruit. What does Minnie like best, or is there any way of telling?"

"Oh, she loves mangoes. Without a doubt, mangoes are her favorite."

Carol told me about having to pay for a twenty-five-dollar stuffed toy Harry snatched from a shelf at the drugstore, and the time he shredded the cushion of a chair, "custom, filled with down. My living room looked as if it had snowed." As she said, "I'll send you a picture," Harry decided he wanted to get back up on the couch. We all looked at each other, anxious. I gave him his boost. This time, Minnie didn't react at all.

We took turns feeding the dogs chicken and hamburger. No sign of jealousy. Good.

I asked Carol about the picture of a fancy, flag-festooned sphere she had at the bottom of all her emails, a kind of logo or family crest. It had a crown at the top, a ribbon with her name, Fertig, on it rippling across the bottom. Each flagpole had a little animal at its tip, a rabbit or a cat or a bird. The

78

standard from some made-up monarchy, I thought, the sort of thing that might be carried at the head of a parade of gargoyles.

Carol explained she liked armorials, insignias that suggest medieval heraldry or coats of arms, so she designed her own whimsical one. "Harry has one, too," she said. His was similar to hers but had a black-and-white bull terrier on top, a cross made out of dog bones dangling from a chain at the bottom. His name appeared as *Sir* Harry Fertig, so I was to understand he was noble and chivalrous. "Ooh, very nice," I told Carol. She promised to make one for Minnie, "*Lady* Minnie Teichner, that is." "For a girl who thinks she's a glamorous movie star or maybe a princess," I said, "it's most fitting."

After a couple of hours, Stephen announced that the visit was over. He had to feed and walk his dog, Teddy. Carol and Harry lived way downtown, Stephen way uptown, which meant that from my apartment, he had to drive the length of Manhattan and then some to drop them off and then get home, an hour and a half for the entire trip, if he happened to be lucky, and the traffic wasn't too bad.

Minnie and I trailed along behind them

as Carol urged Harry in the direction of Stephen's car. Like kremlinology, figuring out what Minnie's actions do or don't mean is a perplexing guessing game. I read it as positive that she wasn't refusing to walk. Harry stopped to do his business. It came out half-formed and bloody. Carol saw me staring at it. Stooping with her pickup bag, she turned to me: "That's his chronic colitis." Not good.

Stephen's old Land Rover was battered and boxlike, in need of a new bumper and a wash. He opened the back to reveal a dog bed. Harry stood on his hind legs, put his front paws on the tailgate, and looked around to see who would lift him up. Late that night Carol emailed me:

August 6, 2016

11:34pm. By the by, Harry slept from when we returned until thirty minutes ago!!!

Xc&H

Sent from heaven
Typos courtesy Apple

I replied:

Sunday, August 7, 2016

6:40 am . . . Dating is exhausting.

Carol:

LOL!!!!!! and so true.

The exchange continued:

To: Martha Teichner
Tuesday, August 9, 2016 5:53 pm
Subject: re: SIR HARRY FERTIG

I confess I have told some dear friends about your email. . . . "Dating is Exhausting." High marks.

Xc

And then, on August 9, 2016, at 5:57 p.m., Martha Teichner wrote:

True for people and dogs.

Wednesday, August 10 . . . Carol came to dinner with Harry but without Stephen. "He offers to drive all the time, but I feel embarrassed because he lives so far away, so we took an Uber." She brought lovely pastries from a French bakery, cooked hamburger, a dented metal bowl, and a tennis ball.

Harry's famous ball and bowl, the very bowl he'd found in a dog park when he was a puppy, looked like what the English call a pudding basin. It was maybe four and a half, five inches high, roughly the same measurement across the top, but rounded, smaller at the bottom. Carol put it on the floor and handed Harry the ball. He immediately plopped it into the bowl, picked the bowl up with his teeth, and started waving it around. When the ball fell out, as it bounced, he used the bowl to catch it, then waved his head around some more till the ball fell out again. Catch and repeat. Catch and repeat. When it seemed we weren't watching him play his game anymore, he came over to me and began jiggling the bowl between his teeth so it made a chattering noise and then nudged me with it. I noticed that his upper and lower fangs were worn down to the level of his other teeth. No wonder. Minnie was standing a few feet away looking puzzled.

Both dogs followed me down the back stairs into the garden when I carried out pork chops to grill on the barbecue. Minnie sniffed Harry from back to front, snuffling loudly as she conducted her inspection. It was the first time she'd shown any curiosity about him. Back inside, Harry asked for a boost onto the couch. Minnie jumped up beside him. There they stayed, together, for an hour or so. Later, Harry became interested in the objects on a table next to the couch: my first two Emmys, a couple of sculptures and some tribal handicrafts I'd bought when I lived in South Africa, a vase, photographs in frames, almost everything breakable. He tried to stand up on his hind legs and knock it all down with his paws. Carol decided he was being annoying and shut him in Minnie's crate for a little time-out. I said, "You know Manhattan Mini Storage?" It's a network of storage-unit rental facilities in old industrial buildings around the city known for corny billboard advertisements such as this one:

"In my father's house there are
many rooms." — John 14:2
Clearly, Jesus was not a New Yorker.

"I call this Manhattan Minnie Storage, *M-I-N-N-I-E*. I should paint a sign."

Carol chuckled but should probably have groaned. During dinner, the dogs lay quietly side by side under the dining table.

We covered a lot of subjects before we got

83

to her cancer. Books we'd both read. TV shows she watched. We seemed to have the same tastes. I have a row of cookbooks on a bench against the wall opposite my table. Carol pulled out one she had, too, and showed me the recipe for a meringue filled with raspberries and cream she made sometimes for dinner parties. I love to cook and cook every day when I'm not traveling, but because I never seem to have much time to experiment, I tend to look at my cookbooks as if they were decorating magazines, for the pictures, feasting my eyes and imagination. The photo of the raspberry meringue looked decadent.

Carol told me she grew up in the New York area, went to art school in Philadelphia, married one of her classmates, and took his name, Fertig. "I was a child bride." They moved to Chicago together and eventually back to Philadelphia before they divorced. She returned to New York. She said she was married a second time, briefly, but didn't elaborate. I told her I'd never been married, although not by choice.

It was easy for me to forget that she was dying. Did she ever forget? She didn't act sick. We were having fun. I liked her. It had been clear to me from her first visit that she was the sort of person I wished I'd known for twenty years, the kind of person I would have wanted as a friend for life. She was interesting. She had an edgy sense of humor. I was curious about her.

Making friends is easier when you're young. People seem to have room in their lives then and the time to make an effort, before their routines, their careers, their families, their obligations, crowd out discovery and make candor unlikely, listening a luxury. But here we were, getting to know each other as if we had all the time in the world, when just the opposite was true. Or maybe it was *because* time was short that we were allowing ourselves to become friends, to laugh, to confide in each other, to experience each moment in extra-sharp focus. If I were waiting to die, would I have the guts to enjoy myself, to accept new friends?

Maybe this is how life is meant to be lived *all* the time, I found myself thinking, before being jolted back to reality. No, if Carol ever forgot she was dying, it was only fleetingly. When she talked about her illness, she couldn't look me in the eye. She looked down and then off to one side as she told me that her liver cancer had metastasized to a tumor on her spine. She was undergoing radiation to shrink the tumor. It had gotten smaller, and she was in less pain. "But really, there is nothing to be done. I'm resigned. It is what it is."

And it could, so easily, have been me. Substitute Martha for Carol. I could have been the one dying of cancer. A single woman, alone, with a beloved dog nobody wanted. Then Minnie would have been facing death, just because. It could still be me someday. I had to consider Carol's "situation" and what to do about Harry with that realization always echoing in my mind. What if it were me?

"Maybe I'll start going to Pilates classes again," she said, looking up. "When I was diagnosed, I stopped everything, but maybe I'll go back. I think exercise is supposed to be good for pain. I'm doing *Object-Lesson* again. I'll keep going as long as I can."

Object-Lesson was her blog. For years, five mornings a week, subscribers woke up to an email from Carol containing a picture of something beautiful with a short reflection on its history and significance, one day a jade necklace, another a dozen embroidered gloves, or maybe a life-size hand made out of porcelain, painted gold. "I'll send you my latest. It's a pair of nineteenth-century, jeweled Chinese finger guards."

"Are you still working?"

She described the tiles she was designing for the ceilings and walls of the lobby bathrooms in a London hotel and charms for a prestigious Madison Avenue jeweler. "Working gives me some purpose. It keeps me sane. Anyway, I need the money. When I don't feel well, I work in bed, or I watch television."

By ten o'clock, Carol looked gray and wilted. She said she was tired and needed to take Harry home. She found his bowl but not his tennis ball. As I walked with her to the street, I said I'd return it. "Don't worry about it. He's got at least thirty," she said as she nudged him into an Uber. "Next time, come to my apartment. I want you to see Harry in his natural habitat."

Sunday, August 14 . . . I came out of the subway at Wall Street. I had Harry's tennis ball and a cold bottle of Montmorency cherry juice in a plastic bag. Some stories have theme songs. This one had a drink. Tart cherry juice from a farm in Leelanau County, maybe ten miles from where I grew up, mixed with sparkling water. To my amazement, I happened on the concentrate at my neighborhood Whole Foods. Naturally, I bought a bottle. I've been buying it ever since. It's good. The first time Carol and Stephen brought Harry inside my apartment, I gave them some. Carol watched me pour the thick liquid into her glass and smiled as dark red swirls bled over the ice into the bubbles. The artist in her approved. "It's beautiful." She loved it, and suddenly it was the next big thing for a woman who had spent her career identifying the next big thing and still, even getting ready to die, couldn't resist something new. We had started our own two-person fad. I sent her home with an extra bottle I had in the fridge. For my first visit to her apartment, I decided to bring her the big twenty-five-dollar bottle. I knew she was having trouble doing her shopping and had run out.

Carol's directions said to turn left when I saw the New York Stock Exchange. On a Sunday afternoon, its grand columns loomed over an empty street, cobbled not paved, barricaded at each end since 9/11, the shadow of a tall building slicing across its light at an angle. Here and there, people posed themselves for selfies. I saw lovers kiss and then look around to see whether people were watching. Police marched a couple of German shepherds back and forth on short leashes. To my right, in full sun, who was standing over me but George Washington in all his glory, a giant bronze

George Washington on a pedestal, at the very spot, or so it's believed, that he was sworn in as the first president of the United States in 1789.

I read Carol's email again. Once I turned left, it said, if I got to Hermès, I had gone too far. Okay. She lived at 15 Broad Street, directly across from the Stock Exchange. I found the door, but because I was early, I cupped my hands around my eyes and looked in the windows of the closed store at the belts and handbags and ties. I got bored, so I tried to call Carol. No answer on her landline. No answer on her cell. I waited and tried again. Still no answer. I stared up the street at George Washington. With his right hand slightly raised, he seemed to be bestowing his benediction on an empty arena, a strange, quiet place on a Sunday, deserted by commerce and its bustle, this spot millions of people visit every year, where billions of dollars change hands. It didn't seem possible that people could actually live here, that they might wave to their neighbors and say hello, but they do. In the distance I saw Carol and Harry passing George, familiar as they ambled my way, as if they were walking down any street in any neighborhood. Carol had a bag from the pharmacy.

In a previous life, 15 Broad Street was the headquarters of JPMorgan, the investment bank. The French designer Philippe Starck turned it into a luxury condominium development. Carol led me through the doors into a tunnel of trendiness. We passed possibly the biggest chandelier I've ever seen. It wasn't hanging down from the ceiling. It was rising up from the floor, like an enormous, gold Christmas tree, dripping with crystals instead of ornaments. The corridor opened out into the kind of lobby you'd expect in a repurposed, former bank building, restyled so that it was over-the-top and minimalist at the same time. A couple of uniformed men looked small behind a gargantuan wooden chest, fancy, like something out of Versailles times ten, marble topped, encrusted with gilt curlicues. It was the reception desk. They waved at Carol and Harry as the three of us made our way to the elevator. Harry was clearly a city boy with a lifetime of experience riding elevators. He walked in, turned around, and calmly faced front just as the other passengers did. Everybody in the car knew him by name and greeted him, which he seemed to like. They chatted with Carol until, one by one, they got off at their respective floors. I've lived in buildings where residents just stare stone-faced at the changing numbers as they go up or down, as if there were a rule that people in elevators are supposed to ignore one another. What did it say that in a huge building with hundreds of apartments, Carol and Harry were known and liked?

Carol's apartment on the tenth floor was bright white, a studio large enough to be called, in real estate speak, a loft. I looked around and thought with relief, She's a maximalist, like me. She had loads of stuff everywhere, interesting stuff that couldn't all be taken in at a glance. By the door, a banquet chair, its seat covered in navy-blue fabric printed with white bull terriers. A pile of cocktail napkins embossed with gold bull terriers on a little cocktail table. A wonderful painting of a woman leaning against a chest of drawers. Pictures halfway down the side of a partition, at eye level if you were sitting. Bookshelves to the ceiling crammed with books. Things I recognized from the *Elle Decor* article: her idea wall relocated to the doors of a wardrobe, a spiky sculpture that looked like a tangle of sea urchins dipped in gold paint. Different apartment, same building. Carol told me the one in the magazine was bigger. She'd been renting it.

When the owner sold it, she moved to this studio.

I felt pulled to the windows at the far end of the room. There were no curtains. Who would want curtains with a view like Carol's? Looking out at layer upon layer of tall buildings from ten stories up was like seeing New York in an IMAX film through 3D glasses. Mesmerizing.

I instantly coveted Carol's dining table, a long, slim marble oval on a pedestal stretching between those windows, more a sculpture than a surface for place mats and salt shakers. Later, I learned it was designed by Eero Saarinen, who was as well-known for Washington Dulles Airport and the Gateway Arch in St. Louis as he was for his furniture.

Most kitchens are square or U-shaped. Carol's lined one wall in the middle of the apartment: sink, dishwasher, stove, counter, refrigerator, all in a row. Instead of cereal boxes or jars of peanut butter, her shelves held designer plates, art objects. Stretched out on the white countertop was a tufty-looking cat she introduced as Bruno, twenty-two years old. Nearby, Harry's crate. Minnie's crate is the kind airlines accept, dull gray plastic with a metal-grid door. Ugly but practical. It's got stickers on it left over from past flights that say LIVE ANIMAL,

THIS SIDE UP, old shipping manifests and baggage tags, some half-torn-off. Harry's, on the other hand, was a fashion statement. A big rectangle on wheels made out of stainless steel wire, inside it had decorated wall panels, on one, his SIR HARRY FERTIG crest blown up and printed in black, on another, a knight, a lady, and a peacock next to a gold sunburst. Spread out on his cushions, an array of toys. Hanging over the open door, a string of painted wooden letters, the kind you'd find hanging over a baby's crib, spelling out HARRY. Carol's bed was a mattress on a platform. It was covered in decorative pillows, disguised as a couch. Slightly sultan's palace.

I found myself wondering what it would be like living there. The place was cool, so cool. I felt a little envious, but why? I have an apartment I love, with two bedrooms, two bathrooms, and a den, two working fireplaces, and a garden, complete with a tree, for heaven's sake. Small, by suburban standards, big for New York City. It's filled with all my belongings and the stories they have to tell. Rugs I've brought back from Middle East war zones, art from my three years in South Africa, antiques from my nine years in England. My apartment has appreciated so much in value that if I were moving to New York now, I couldn't afford it. Why would I even speculate about life in Carol's studio apartment? I realized it was her taste, her artist's eye, that made it so enticing.

She had on a slightly shiny, gauzy black dress. Her design? Vintage? It was sleeveless, so her pain patch showed. The dress looked Greek or Roman, as if she'd stepped out of the antiquities hall at the Metropolitan Museum. She wore it with a cord belted at the waist, flat sandals, and a narrow black leather band wrapped triple around her wrist as a bracelet. She seemed to wear a lot of black, but then I do, too. It's New York.

She got a bottle of rosé out of the fridge, opened it, and carried it over to her beautiful dining table along with two small glasses, delicate, old looking, surrounded by fine lines of beading. The cheese board she put down next had two small cheeses on it, one round, one square, some dried cranberries, a mound of raw almonds, and a few plain crackers, all placed exactly the same distance apart in an elegant line. We drank to bull terriers. Harry came over to me and thrust his bowl and ball into my lap, chattered his teeth on the metal, wanting me to play with him. He had a different bowl from the one Carol had brought to my apartment. This one was shallower and wider, with room enough for more tennis balls. I put it on his head and said it would make a nice World War I helmet should he need one.

What Carol told me as we sat eating the perfectly runny cheese, talking about her work, startled me. "Fashion is unbelievably aggressive and competitive. It's brash and ruthless. It's coarse and rude," she said, "but magazine publishing is worse. It's more polite on the surface but much, much more treacherous. I prefer working for myself." So her career hadn't just been smooth sailing, success after success. The anger, the implied hurt she wasn't explaining. I wondered who had disappointed her, and where cancer fit in her sense of how her life had gone. For all her wit and sophistication, she had an innocence about her, a vulnerability. I began to see that Carol lived for art and beauty at her own peril. No matter what the cost, she couldn't help herself.

She said she wanted to lend me a book about the death of luxury. We'd been moaning about how a designer label slapped on a garment made sloppily in China devalued that label, how it was no wonder department stores were going out of business when they'd all been renamed Macy's and sold the same merchandise. So why not just go for markdowns? She got up from the table and went to her bookshelves. Instead of looking up at the books, she looked down at the various gatherings of her belongings leaning against nearby furniture. Finally she found what she was looking for and brandished it over her head like a sword. "This was my last year's Secret Santa present in the building," she said, smiling. It was a grabber, by far the best grabber I had ever seen, with a sturdy trigger-grip handle, a nice long reach, and wide, rubberized duck-bill pincers. I wondered who in her building had thought of such a practical present. "I have a grabber," I said, "but it's not nearly that nice. I had my hips replaced about ten years ago. The hospital gave me one after the surgery, but I had to get a second one, to pick up the first one, because it kept falling over. Goose chewed one of them up."

Carol laughed loudly as she used hers to extract the book from the top shelf and handed it to me. "I want to show you something." She led me to her laptop, which was open on top of a trunk that she had placed on her desk. I guessed that working standing up instead of sitting down hurt her back less where she'd had radiation. After a few clicks, she said, "Look." What was on her screen looked like an extreme close-up of the inside of a terrarium. It was vivid and green, jungly, dense with ferns and trailing vines and lacy, fine-veined leaves, dotted with insects and butterflies and blossoms, each detail distinct and hyperreal. "This is for the women's bathroom in the Morgans hotel, for the tiles I'm working on." Then she showed me the design for the men's room. Same idea, but no insects and butterflies. They were wonderful and hypnotic. I could imagine people going into those bathrooms and not wanting to come out. God help anyone under the influence of a controlled substance. Or a bit drunk. I vowed right then and there to go and visit the hotel on my next trip to London to see at least the women's bathroom for myself.

Carol said, "I'm not going to show you the armorial for Minnie. It's not done yet." But, of course, she did. I said I was reminded of when I was little and would get so excited about the Christmas presents I'd made or bought for my parents that I couldn't help showing them before Christmas. I always asked them to forget about what they'd seen.

Minnie's crest matched Harry's, sort of. A rippling banner across the bottom said LADY MINNIE TEICHNER instead of SIR HARRY FERTIG. Like Harry's, hers had crossed bones hanging from a chain. Harry straddled a large crown. Ms. Minnie Herself, as I call her, was perched on a bed of flowers and, like Harry, was surrounded by ceremonial flags topped with cute little animals. But unlike Harry, Minnie was wearing something on her head. I looked and saw it was a kind of dog tiara, trimmed with three grand, Victorian-looking ostrich-feather plumes. "Just her style," I said. "That's fabulous." Snowflakes and stars and flowers decorated the circle in the center of Harry's. Carol called it "the roundel." Minnie's roundel had a tree in it and what . . . a mango? "Yes," Carol said. "You said she liked mangoes." I couldn't stop laughing.

I looked at my watch and realized the afternoon was almost gone. I told Carol I needed to start thinking about getting home to feed Minnie. "I should show you how I feed Harry," she said, stalling. She mixed two kinds of prescription diet dry food together, one for delicate stomachs, the other for fiber. She kneaded his various pills into wads of prescription canned food, including a couple of yellowish capsules she said were for his colitis. "Tylan." Right, the capsules she made with her capsule machine while watching *CBS Sunday Morning.* "Next time, I'll give you a lesson."

Harry gobbled up his food. "We'll go out when you leave, but first I want you to see how we play." Carol attached his leash, then collected pickup bags, her keys, and Harry's World War I helmet bowl. We took the elevator down to some sort of nether floor, to a semi-basement below the lobby. It was a large space, empty, apparently unused. Carol unhooked Harry. He looked at her, clearly expecting something to happen. She took his bowl and flung it as if it were a Frisbee. It clattered on the concrete floor. Harry bounded after it, pushed it to a corner with his nose, picked it up, wiggled it, then ran back to Carol and me. He tried to taunt us into grabbing it from him. Carol threw it for him again and again. He skidded against walls and banged the bowl around, making as much noise with it as he could and seemed happy. After about fifteen minutes, he abruptly lay down, the bowl still in his mouth. "Okay, he's done," Carol announced. "That's what he does when he gets tired out. I try to give him a workout like this every day."

We took Harry outside. Carol handed me his leash. "I want you to walk him." He cooperated, stopping to do another runny, bloody big business. I cleaned it up. When we got to the subway stop, Wall Street again,

I handed the leash back. Carol and I agreed to do dinner again the following Wednesday, August 17. I gave Harry a kiss on the top of his head and waved goodbye.

Six:
The New Normal

Wednesday, August 17, 2016. I mixed all the dry ingredients for the peach crisp in the morning before I went to work. My intention was to leave the office early, at five instead of seven, so that I could get the peaches cut up and the dessert baked before Carol and Harry arrived. Carol said she would bring a rotisserie chicken from Eataly, an Italian market and food hall located in one of the new World Trade Center buildings built after 9/11, not far from where she lived. It is, no exaggeration, a palace of edible overload. "They brine them for six hours," Carol told me when she offered to go and get a chicken for our dinner. "They're the best chickens I've ever had. Really juicy." Where food is concerned, New York is all about knowing where to get the good stuff. By late morning, we were emailing each other and joking about Harry stealing the chicken.

At about five-fifteen, as the bus inched down Ninth Avenue, my cell phone rang. It was Carol. She, too, was on a bus, headed home. Between the noise of her bus and mine, I could barely hear her. "I've got the chicken," I made out, "but it's been a very difficult day." Her voice was faint and sounded sad. She seemed to be pleading, not asking, "Please, do you think we could postpone dinner till tomorrow night? It's been so . . . tiring . . . today. I'm exhausted. I need to go home and go to bed. I'm so, so sorry." I said, "Sure, fine. I hope you feel better. Get some sleep." The playful emails, then the plaintive phone call. My answering machine was blinking when I got home. Same message. Same tone of voice. For the rest of the evening I felt rattled, not quite sure what to do with myself. I've never erased her message.

In the morning, Carol let me know she felt better, rested enough to come to dinner with Harry. She arrived that night with a large carrier bag. First, she lifted out the chicken, then mango slices for Minnie, who refused to take them from her. How impolite. Next, she produced Harry's bowl and enough tennis balls to keep a juggler happy, but he paid no attention and went straight to the kitchen, where, he remembered, the treats were kept. Also impolite. Carol and I laughed. For me, she had a pad of place mats. "For your place in South Carolina," she said.

I had never seen anything like it before. It was something she had designed.

The label said:

Carol Fertig's HAPPY
50 SHEETS
Paper Placemats on a Pad.

And in the lower left-hand corner:

Made in the U.S. of A.

The place mats were gold, covered with branches of coral in black and white. The look was a little more beach house than I would have chosen, but then she didn't know that my home in South Carolina doesn't look like a beach house. The idea was fabulous and ingenious. You tear one off, use it, then throw it away.

At dinner, Carol told me she had gotten herself overtired the day before. "I've always been a really active person. I haven't slowed down. I haven't really acknowledged I'm sick. I have to learn to pace myself, scale back." She sighed. "It's the new normal, I guess." Each little capitulation to her cancer, I thought, is a step closer to the end, and she knows it.

She'd been to her pain doctor to try to figure out whether she could lower the dosage of her pain medication. "I don't want to rely on it till I have to." She told me, for the second or third time since I'd met her, "I think I'll go back to Pilates. The doctor said it would be good for relieving stress, and that will help with the pain. He suggested yoga, but I told him I'm not a yoga person." She wanted to go back to Pilates. Wishful thinking, I suspected. I doubted she could. She admitted, "I don't know how to deal with stress. Before this, I'd have a vodka martini, but now I don't know what to do." I said, "Coming home at night and listening to audiobooks while I cook is one way I deal with stress, and taking my dogs to the Hudson River early in the morning. My job can be very, very stressful, but it's not the same as the stress you're feeling." I was thinking about how she felt facing her cancer, but I came to believe that she had always internalized stress and that anxiety was a constant in her life.

"The hotel people are driving me crazy," she said. "The woman I have to deal with in London, she's maybe, *maybe* twenty-five.

She's unbelievably disrespectful, officious. There's no courtesy, no deference to my work. I'm a consultant, not a servant. She's dictatorial, makes pronouncements. I've gotten my designs back with arrows across them and orders in the margin. *Move this flower . . . here!*" Carol pointed. "Never, *please move the flower.*" She held up an arm as if she were about to do a "Friends, Romans, countrymen" declamation. "The men's room is supposed to be" — here Carol parodied the woman's English accent — "a totally green moment." I laughed. "That's the kind of pretentious nonsense people throw around in art school," she said, then sighed again. I remembered the beautiful green images I'd seen on her laptop.

"I think I'm taking out my anger about being sick on this project. I hate these people, but it's worse because, really, I'm angry about other things." I asked what was left to do, when the job would be finished. "Monday. I told them I was going away, even though I'm not, and that it had to be done by Monday. All that's left is a little cleanup, which my assistant will have to do anyway." Carol looked at me with a sly smile. "Then I'll just have to get upset about some other project."

We talked about clothes, what we liked, what we didn't like. I showed her a dressy black jacket I'd bought a few months before. She admired it and said casually, "I have the perfect bag for that jacket." I took the comment to mean we liked the same sorts of things. We moved on to other topics.

Carol thought that leaving Harry with me for a few hours would be a good idea. "I could drop him off and go to the movies or have lunch. Eventually we should both go somewhere and leave the dogs alone together. Do you have a doggy cam?"

A doggy cam, hmmm, so we could spy on our dogs. "No, but I know where to find out about them." I'd been working with a producer and camera crew on a story about dog behavior. To illustrate scientific research about canine smell, we'd gathered a roomful of people's pets, a reluctant Minnie among them, and shot video of these dogs using their noses: sniffing each other, sniffing for hidden treats, sniffing the door to find a way to escape (Minnie).

We also wanted to explore what dogs do when their owners aren't around, so we paid BarkBox a visit.

Subscribe to BarkBox, and every month your dog receives a box full of toys and treats, *themed* toys and treats, such as

106

Chewrassic Bark (dinosaur included) or the Knights of the Hound Table (dragon included). Ridiculously indulgent? Need I ask? BarkBox has something like six hundred thousand subscribers.

Its offices are on New York's Lower East Side at the edge of Chinatown. In one of those seriously cool, remodeled industrial buildings with huge, open loft spaces and pale hardwood floors, the company seems to employ mostly people under the age of thirty-five, many of whom bring their dogs to work. There are walls covered with what look like carpeted cliff dwellings, where employees can nestle in with their pets and work on their laptops at the same time.

For employees whose dogs are too big to haul in to work every day or who are uncomfortable trying to pass their pets off as service animals to get them onto buses and subways, there is the doggy cam. At Bark-Box, desks are placed side by side in long, double rows with identical computer consoles. On many, smartphones and tablet computers are propped behind keyboards, streaming images of dogs doing such interesting things as drinking water, sitting on couches, or sleeping. I watched as workers in need of a dog fix leaned toward the built-in microphones on their devices and called their dogs' names or jabbered baby talk.

Surely, the people at BarkBox, people after my own heart, would know what kind of doggy cam to buy. I said I would make inquiries.

Carol and I ate the chicken she brought, perfect farmers market tomatoes with mozzarella and basil, corn on the cob, and peach crisp. Carol said it was the perfect summer dinner. Minnie sat under the table. Harry spent some time in Manhattan Minnie Storage, aka Minnie's crate. At the end of the meal, we lured both dogs into the kitchen. Their mouths were inches apart as we took turns handing them pieces of chicken, worried at first we were risking a fight. Goose would have tried to snatch Minnie's share. Harry didn't. The two of them ate in peace. Carol and I had a very good time feeding them.

On Saturday, August 27, Stephen and Carol arrived with Harry and her usual large carrier bag full of Harry's belongings and supplies, including his bowl and ball and shriveled pieces of roasted sweet potato. Carol immediately announced, "Nothing for Harry. I created a monster by associating treats with coming here." Then why did she bring sweet potato treats? Maybe she didn't mean it.

I couldn't help but notice her outfit, singular even by her standards. She was wearing a white eyelet A-line skirt; a black top; white, fifties-movie-star-style cat's-eye sunglasses, and a turned-down sailor hat. The hat was covered with silly-looking, grinning cats in several different bright colors.

She told me she thought my garden would be the ideal place to throw Harry's bowl for him to chase and, like the mother of a toddler with separation anxiety, suggested that I keep him busy as she and Stephen slunk out the door, which I did. Just like babysitting in high school.

Harry didn't think my garden was such a good place to chase his bowl. Apparently, he preferred concrete to bumpy, mossy bricks. Metal on concrete makes much more noise. He looked up at me and opened his mouth. His bowl fell out and landed with a bonk. He walked off. What interested him was the gap between the shed where I keep my garbage cans and tools and the fence dividing my garden from my downstairs neighbor's. The space is ten inches wide. I measured it. In Harry went, or half of him. The front half. The back half stuck out, tail wagging. As I watched, wondering whether he was stuck, his left hind leg went up, and a perfectly aimed stream of pee watered the corner of my shed. Seeing a whole dog pee isn't funny. Seeing half a dog pee is hilarious. I laughed out loud as he wriggled himself free.

Back in the apartment, Harry went straight to my bathroom for a drink out of the toilet. He jiggled his bowl and ball. He picked up a pull toy and made me play tug-of-war. He went to the kitchen and, knowing that Minnie's favorite lamb-lung treats were on the counter, barked, expecting me to hurry in and hand over a few. When I told him no, he headed for the dining table and tried to snatch the bag of sweet potato treats Carol had left. He was relentless. In the end I capitulated. I gave him one and then took one to Minnie, who had been watching the action from the couch. I didn't want her to get jealous, so I alternated between the two dogs. I snuggled with her and then played with Harry, snuggled with her, then played with Harry.

As I bounced between them, the phone rang. It was Carol. She and Stephen had stopped for iced tea. Did I want some? I thought to myself, The real reason you're phoning is to check on how things are going, just like a worried mom calling the babysitter. I'd had my share of those calls in high school. I reported and hung up.

Suddenly, Minnie leaped off the couch and flung herself at Harry's feet, dancing and bowing, launching into all her play moves, the twists and dives and feints. Harry stopped jiggling his bowl, stared at her for a second or two, then joined the game. They wrestled and chased each other, tearing back and forth, crashing into furniture. I wanted to referee to make sure they didn't fight, but I also wanted to take pictures. Damn . . . this was quite a show. Carol and Stephen had to see it. I grabbed my cell phone, switched it from photo to video, and began shooting, or so I thought. Unfortunately, I turned the camera off instead of on. I ended up with about two seconds of the dogs disappearing out of the frame. Damn, damn, damn . . .

But what a breakthrough! Harry and Minnie playing with each other. When Carol and Stephen got back, I told them what had happened. I described how Minnie had slid under the dining table, how she'd taunted Harry from behind the chairs. He'd seemed confounded because he couldn't quite figure out how to get at her until I pulled a chair away, and she blasted out across the room. Carol and Stephen were so excited, you'd think I'd been describing a baby's first steps. I kept apologizing for screwing up the video. "Next time," Carol said, and the conversation turned back to doggy cams.

Minnie had, evidently, maxed out on sociability. When Carol and Stephen and Harry left, she refused to follow them out. After they'd gone, I gathered up an armload of clothes to take to the cleaner's. As I turned down Ninth Avenue, Stephen's car passed me. Carol had the window rolled down. She waved wildly. I saw the big smile, the cat's-eye sunglasses, the silly cat hat, and that the whole front bumper of Stephen's old Land Rover was held on with duct tape.

Stephen's email read, "It would mean a lot to Carol if you can join us and meet some of her friends." He was inviting me to a party on the roof of the building where Carol had lived for seventeen years before moving to 15 Broad Street after 9/11. I was touched to be included. For Carol and her pals, the party was a summer tradition, a July event that had slipped to a Sunday night in September in part because of Carol's cancer. Stephen offered to drive me. He was also picking up another guest, Ann King, who lived around the corner from me on Twenty-third Street. When he showed up more or less on time, she declared it a miracle.

Picture a game of pool or pinball, one ball hitting another, setting in motion a chain reaction of balls colliding with one another. Ann King's connections to Stephen and Carol and the other people attending the party reminded me of all those collisions. Typical New York City. It's a small town really. A tall, vigorous Englishwoman with thick white hair and a plummy accent, Ann King had had an interesting career trajectory. Once a model, she moved into the design world and found herself working at the big-name architecture firm where Stephen was also working. They became friends. He was in charge of a team designing boutiques for Calvin Klein. Carol was working for Calvin Klein as a consultant. Stephen and Carol met, immediately hit it off, and became friends for life, except when they were squabbling. Through Stephen, Carol met Ann King, who left the architecture firm and went to work for *Time* magazine, where she met Mary Corliss, the person hosting the party. She knew Carol because they both lived in the same building. Six degrees of separation or, I guess in this case, three or four maybe.

As Ann King was introduced to me, she said, "I think it's wonderful that you're taking Harry." I thought, Wait a minute, *maybe* taking Harry. I said, "Well, it's likely but not a certainty yet," but I don't think she heard me. Stephen was, by that time, explaining that where we were going, 55 Hudson Street, in Tribeca, once was the headquarters of American Express before being turned into apartments. The building was redbrick, handsome but not conspicuous, on a corner. It must have been considered tall when it was built at the end of the nineteenth century, not now.

Carol arrived just as we did. She wore a long, black jersey-knit dress that fell so that it looked as if it were all vertical lines. It was loose with slits for her arms and, like everything else she wore, distinctive, chic. Her hair, makeup, and lipstick were, as usual, perfect, but something, a pallor, a tightness around her eyes, made me think she didn't feel well, that her smile took work.

More people arrived. We were an elevatorful when we got off on Mary Corliss's floor and rang her bell. She greeted us and added what each of us had brought to the tidy row of dishes she'd laid out in her kitchen. "I'm so glad you could make it. It's great that

114

you're taking Harry," she said as she got to me. Where had I heard that before? "It looks fairly certain it's going to happen." I wondered what Carol had told her friends and when.

The gathering was wearing a brave face. Mary Corliss was just beginning to put her life back together. Her husband, Richard Corliss, *Time* magazine's movie critic for thirty-five years, had died of a stroke not quite a year and a half before. Mary is tiny and smart, a film historian and movie critic in her own right. As she made her way around the circle of her guests, I heard her explaining how she hadn't been doing X, Y, or Z, but was trying to start again, to entertain, to go on trips, to see plays.

Carol took me on a tour of the apartment. It was filled with good American art deco and midcentury modern furniture, silver, rugs, lamps. Normally I find rooms decorated in this particular style pretentious and self-conscious. Not here. Mary's apartment was lovely, lived in, and sophisticated, cluttered with evidence that its occupants did a lot of reading and thinking in it. Richard Corliss's study had been left as it was when he was alive. His desk looked as if he were in the middle of something and would be right back. Bookshelves were everywhere, filled not just with books but also with DVDs, probably thousands of them, movies the Corlisses had reviewed or just loved. Mary had her own study, which had not been cleared of work for the occasion. She had opened a shop nearby, Carol told me, which sold the same sort of furniture and accessories she had in the apartment.

"And look at this," Carol said as she led me into a large, sleek bathroom that would have been right at home in a large, sleek restaurant, except it had a luxurious glassed-in shower. Carol clearly loved showing off Mary's apartment. The designer in her couldn't resist. She was smiling, the look I'd spotted earlier gone. I couldn't help but think about the secrets behind the facades of New York City's old buildings, behind all those secret doors, and how sometimes I got to peek inside, as if I were peering at a lit-up stage set from the wings, eavesdropping on a fantasy New York.

Mary pointed in the direction of her kitchen counter. Each of us picked up a platter or dish, bottles of wine, glasses, silverware. We paraded down the hall behind her to the elevator, got out at the top floor, climbed a flight of fire stairs, and took turns holding a metal door, as one by one we maneuvered our little movable feast out onto the roof.

I was completely unprepared for what I saw, how big the space was, how lush the garden, how extraordinary the view. There were chairs and tables and planters overflowing with the last blooms of summer, pink and yellow and purple, slightly leggy, the edges of their leaves just starting to turn brown. Mary had, for years, maintained the garden for the building as a labor of love. She apologized to us that she hadn't quite kept up with it that summer. The reason remained unspoken.

I felt as if I were standing on a platform suspended in the middle of that kind of 3D urban landscape I'd seen through the windows in Carol's apartment, except I was outside. The sky was huge and pale. Dusk was gathering. The weather forecast had been for rain, but the rain hadn't come. Instead, as evening approached, the clouds thinned into streaks and drifted away.

From time to time, traveling as part of my job, I've found myself on an airplane taking off or landing in that same half-light. I've watched other planes gliding by as they taxied to or from their gates, their windows lit from within, white, like neat rows of pearly teeth. From a few hundred feet up I've been able to see into a house or an apartment and make out people at their dinner tables or watching television, sometimes together, sometimes alone, living their lives framed in the rectangles of electric brightness that separated them from the gloom. The 360-degree view from this roof terrace was exponentially more vivid. Behind us, skyscrapers glittered as lights in thousands of windows winked on, like diamonds, like eyes. In front of us as we sat and ate, and darkness closed in, an unearthly, spotlit brilliance rose from below us, like the glow of an inner fire throwing its weird gleam onto the new buildings at the born-again World Trade Center site, a few blocks away.

Every New Yorker who's lived in the city for any length of time has a 9/11 story. I have friends who were right there, next to the Twin Towers, when they saw and heard the first plane hit, others who walked miles covered in ash carrying briefcases, dragging suitcases, barefoot. By chance, CBS News had camera crews nearby, covering something normal, whatever it was, inconsequential and forgotten after 8:46 A.M. There was a primary election that perfect, blue-sky Tuesday. Maybe that was what they were shooting. Their jerky pictures of what looked like ghosts staggering out of the smoke, of strange shapes and bloody shirts and moving chaos, told the story of how they did their jobs as they ran for their lives when the towers fell. The noise on that raw video is almost unbearable to hear.

This is what I know about Carol's 9/11 story, mainly from Stephen. She was at an early-morning meeting at a building full of galleries and design firms on Fifty-seventh Street at Madison Avenue. Stephen had an office in the building, too. When Carol heard about the second plane, she went to find him. He said she was panicky. Her dog, Violet, was in her apartment. They both knew how close it was to Ground Zero. Driving there wasn't possible, so she walked, more than four miles, talked her way past the National Guard, rescued Violet, then walked back uptown to a friend's apartment on East Eighty-second Street, nearly seven miles. It was two weeks before she was allowed to go home. She found everything covered with soot and filth. She cleaned, but the gunk kept seeping in. The fires at Ground Zero burned for a hundred days, and anyone who lived or worked in the area coughed and choked in the smoky haze that hung over Lower Manhattan for months. Environmental Protection Agency reports that the air was safe turned out to be wrong, but it would be years before the poison people breathed in would start killing them. In Carol's case, fifteen years.

That night on the roof was intoxicating — the light, the velvety warmth, the Sunday sounds of the city just soft white noise up so high — but no one there could forget that this would be the last of these parties Carol would attend. She ate very little, and when the rest of us had settled back, pausing before dessert, she announced she didn't feel well and went home.

There was a long silence in the void she left. Finally, the person sitting to my right, a filmmaker named Alan Wade, turned to me and remarked, "It's so good that you're taking Harry." I said nothing.

On Saturday, September 17, Harry and Minnie's next date, Carol emailed that Stephen, surprise, surprise, was running late. They would not be arriving at three P.M. as planned. They showed up just before four. Carol was *dressed.* She wore a sleek, long-sleeved, black cable-knit sweater, black pants, and faux-alligator patent leather flats with tassels. She looked great: carefully groomed, her makeup just so, her lipstick bright red, perfectly applied. She knew how to rise to occasions, I thought. I wondered how she actually felt.

As we settled down to our sparkling water with cherry concentrate, Carol said, "I've got something for you." Her fingers shaking more than I'd seen before, she reached in her ever-present carryall, full of strange things, very Mary Poppins. She pulled out a drawstring pouch and handed it to me. It was corduroy, nearly black, lined in red. I opened it and saw a little lead bull terrier, a couple of inches long. Like an antique toy soldier, I thought. Once upon a time, it had been white, but the paint had peeled and worn, so the finish was patchy. Part of its tail had broken off. There was a tiny dot of red in each eye. It was wonderful, old, and made me think of a well-loved stuffed animal. Carol said, "I've had this so long, I don't even remember where I got it. Maybe Paris, when Violet was alive." I pictured her in Paris, cruising up and down the aisles of the famous flea market, knowing style when she saw it. I thanked her, hoping she realized how fully I understood her gift and valued it. She had given away, given to me, another of her treasures.

Harry wasn't himself. One of the pads on his right front foot had split. He was limping badly and in pain. He didn't want to play, not even with his bowl and ball. Carol asked me whether I had one of those awful

Elizabethan collars vets put on dogs to keep them from licking wounds. I did, two in fact, one hard, clear plastic, the miserable kind, the other soft and a little floppy, made out of some sort of blue, coated cloth divided into sections. When Minnie wore it, she looked like a petunia. Carol chose that one, held it over Harry, and said dramatically, "The cone of shame."

We chatted for a while, then Carol told Stephen to take Harry out in the garden. "Go, go!" She waved her hand toward the back door. It took him a minute to understand that she wanted to tell me something.

First, she said that the following Saturday was Stephen's birthday. When they brought Harry over, she wanted to surprise him with a cake. Easy, I thought. She always brought her bag full of Harry's stuff. She could hide anything in it. I said I would have plates and forks ready.

Then she told me that she'd had a rough week. On Monday she'd gone to her lawyer's office "to get my affairs in order . . . so I don't leave my friends with . . . a mess." Next, she went to four of her doctors, one of them three different times. I asked her what sort of doctors. "My GP, my palliative-care doctor, my shrink, and a psychopharmacologist." I had never heard of psychopharmacology. Later I looked it up and discovered that it's the study of how drugs affect mood, sensation, thinking, and behavior. Carol said the psychopharmacologist was working with the palliative-care doctor to improve her quality of life.

"In my GP's office, I was crying and crying. I love him. I've known him for years. I was telling him about going to the lawyer. He said, 'Try to look at this another way. Your friends may need to go through your things and settle your affairs to help them grieve.' I told him I have no joy in my life right now. It's too much. I'm just tired, exhausted all the time. So he told me, 'Every day, do something that brings you joy.' " I asked her what she'd been doing. "Now," she said, "every day I lie down on the floor next to Harry. I stay there with him and pet him. That brings me joy."

The psychopharmacologist, she said, had prescribed a drug called Wellbutrin, an antidepressant that apparently helps people with their energy level. "I think it's beginning to help, but being tired all the time is really upsetting me, me, the girl who always did fifteen things a day."

As she said all of this, she looked away, as she had when she'd first told me about her cancer. She couldn't ever meet my eyes when she discussed her "situation."

"I've asked the lawyers. . . . I've put aside money for you to take care of Harry." At first I said nothing. I had never actually told her I would take Harry. We were planning to leave the dogs alone together and then to try sleepovers. Harry and Minnie were getting along, but there were still risks, I thought, more tests to pass. For Carol, though, it was a done deal. She was sure. Until then, my position had been I would take him *if* all continued to go well. From that moment on, it was, *yes,* I would take him unless something disastrous happened.

I said, "You don't have to. . . . It's not necessary."

She looked at me. "I know. . . . I need to." She sighed. "When something happens to him, if there's any left, please give it to the Bull Terrier Club of America rescue fund."

I nodded. "Of course." She didn't say how much she was leaving. I didn't ask. Knowing that she was having trouble paying her bills, I wondered where the money would come from, whether it even existed. She had applied to what was then the more than $7 billion 9/11 Victim Compensation Fund, authorized by Congress to help individuals or the families of individuals who had gotten sick or died because of their exposure to the toxic haze at Ground Zero, both first responders and private citizens. An administrator called a special master was appointed to determine who qualified for compensation and how much each payout would be, according to a complicated calculus based on lifetime earning potential, degree of pain and suffering, number of dependents, and other factors. In other words, a formula to decide how much a life is worth. Each time the deadline for applying has been close to expiring, it's been extended, and Congress has agreed to replenish the fund, so it won't run out.

Carol's doctors were sure her cancer was the result of living near Ground Zero. Her lawyers were optimistic her claim would be approved, but how much she'd get and when, they had no idea.

When Stephen came back inside with the dogs, Carol suggested leaving me alone with them again. Harry and Minnie lay by the back door catching the breeze from the garden, sleeping side by side with their front paws intertwined, apparently unaware that Carol and Stephen had gone for a walk.

Harry didn't know it, but I had plans for him in their absence. I rummaged around in a cupboard until I found nonstick gauze squares, stretchy tape, antibiotic ointment, and cotton pads. I have a stash of dog snow booties in at least four sizes. I picked one I thought might fit Harry and filled a pot with warm water and a slug of iodine. Shaking Minnie's treat bag under his nose, I woke him up and lured him, limping, into the kitchen. I put his painful foot in the pot to soak and stood back, expecting him to knock the pot over, splashing water everywhere. He didn't. He just stood there. So far so good. I washed his toes with soap, rinsed, and dried them. I made a little stack of cotton pads and topped it with a gauze square, then squeezed out a little worm of antibiotic ointment on it, held it under Harry's paw, and was just wrapping the stretchy tape around it when the doorbell rang. As I buzzed Carol and Stephen into the building, Harry got loose. His bandage completely unraveled. He was trailing the whole roll of tape after him as he went to the door, and it only got worse when he discovered who was there. The tape got tangled up between his feet as he greeted the two of them. With Stephen's help holding the squirming dog, I retrieved the tape, rerolled it, and tried again, but only managed to tape Stephen's finger to Harry's foot. When I finally got the bandage and bootie on, Harry stepped down on the floor, realized that his foot didn't hurt, and immediately started to romp and play. He was a dog transformed. We were all amazed to see the immediate difference in him, once he could put weight on his foot without pain. Wearing his bootie, he reminded me of Michael Jackson wearing one glove. I explained that in the last few months of Piggy's life, one of his pads had cracked, too, and wouldn't heal. Every day, I did the same thing for him.

As Stephen and Carol got ready to leave, Stephen announced, "Next Saturday is my fifty-eighth birthday." Carol and I glanced at each other. Stephen pulled up his shirt a little. "I guess it's a sign of my age. I've developed a paunch." He stuck out his stomach as if he had a basketball in it. "I always had a six-pack. The paunch is something new, just in the last few months." I said I was sixty-eight. I asked Carol how old she was. She said, "Oh, I never tell anyone," then immediately told us she was seventy. Stephen seemed startled. "You should have said something. I would have had a party." Carol laughed. "Stop talking and take me home, please." I handed her another big bottle of cherry concentrate. She seemed a bit disoriented as she tried to figure out what she needed to gather up . . .

the cherry juice, the bowl and balls, the petunia cone of shame, her purse.

A happy Harry, walking without a limp, led the way out to the street. I followed with an unhappy Minnie, who did not want to go out. As she locked her legs and lowered her head in protest, Stephen pointed out the low-slung Tesla sports car parked directly in front of my stoop. Bright orange, jack-o'-lantern colored. "Really ugly," he said. "If anyone wanted to see how old I am, all they'd have to do is watch me try and get into a car like that." Carol's retort, "No, all they'd have to do is see you try to get out."

SEVEN:
A PERFECT ENGLISH TEA

The minute I set foot in a big electronics box store, I'm like a deer in the headlights. Those rows and rows of televisions, inches apart, assault my eyes with way-too-bright pictures of skiers or something, the same skier slaloming down the same mountain at the same time on dozens and dozens of screens, tiny on the twenty-four-inch models, enormous on the home-theater-size models. It's like being in a surreal, HD hall of mirrors, my vision of hell.

The doggy cams were right next to the TVs.

Why was I even in one of those stores? An invitation to tea. The night of the party on the roof, Carol had told Ann King that the next step with Minnie and Harry was to leave them alone together and that we wanted to get a doggy cam so that wherever we went, we could watch them, spy on them, to see what they would do. We had to pick a spot not too far away, so that if they started to fight, we could get back before they killed each other. Ann said, "Come to tea!" She reminded Carol that she lived right around the corner from me. "Sunday, two weeks from now, anytime after three." The only problem was, we didn't have a doggy cam.

The BarkBox people had recommended several brands for different reasons: price, picture quality, ease of operation. The salesman, when I finally found one, took me through the features of each type. I said, "I need *really* easy." He pointed me toward the most expensive one. "It's very simple." His description of how it worked seemed intuitive enough. *Easy to use* was written all over the packaging, but I worry about such claims.

At the very beginning of my CBS career, through the winter of 1978, I covered a national strike by coal miners. I spent three months in the Appalachian "hollers" of West Virginia, eastern Kentucky, and southern Ohio, which are notorious for their winding, unmarked roads. Finding your way around, if you're not from there, isn't easy even now. Then, before GPS devices or Google Maps, it was ridiculous. You'd ask somebody for directions, and the person would start rattling off a list of left turns, right turns, by this creek or that house with a recliner on the front porch, or a field with a horse in it. At the end of one of those convoluted recitations, the direction giver invariably said with a smile, "Cain't miss it." And invariably you'd get lost.

So, when I heard, "Easy," I was suspicious, but being over twenty-five and tech tentative, I had to rely on somebody. As far as easy was concerned, I was easy prey. I went home with the expensive model. I emailed Carol that I had it. About getting it working, her advice was "Let Stephen figure it out. He knows how to do that sort of thing."

The following Saturday, when Carol arrived with Harry, she brought a Mary Poppins carryall with her as usual, but this one was unusually large. While Stephen tried to find a parking space, she unloaded Harry's bowl and balls, a supply of cut-up pieces of chicken, a thumb drive with Minnie's armorial on it, a mysterious orange Hermès gift box, a plastic bag filled with something that made a rustling noise, a pint of vanilla ice cream, and a cherry pie. She explained that Stephen preferred birthday pie to birthday cake. She'd emailed me to have the oven on warm, so she stashed the pie in the oven and the ice cream in the freezer. I'd gone birthday-candle shopping a few nights before. I went to three different places and bought five different kinds for Carol to consider.

When Stephen arrived, she put him to work on the doggy cam setup. He downloaded the app onto my phone and Carol's. That seemed to work. Nothing else did. Weren't we the picture of middle-aged, baby-boomer technological incompetence, proof that stereotypes can be accurate? Except that Stephen really did know what he was doing where computers were concerned. Even figuring out what password the app and the computer required confounded us. The underside of my modem had a string of letters and numbers listed as password, but of course that wasn't it. What the app wanted was another list of numbers called the WEP key. Carol and I took turns reading the directions to Stephen, who uttered strange grunts and bleats as he tried to figure out what the words meant. An hour into this losing battle, we started phoning customer service lines, which involved navigating multiple menus and enduring long waits on hold, first with the company that was my internet/phone provider, then Nest, the maker of the doggy cam. We tried moving the modem from its usual home in my au pair's bedroom to the living room. After more than two hours of trying, the best picture we were able to get was a freeze frame of my living room or pixilation, not streaming video of Harry and Minnie. Carol and I watched as Stephen lost patience. His grunts and bleats turned into sighs. Soon his sighs turned into swear words.

Finally, we gave up. Carol studied the birthday-candle choices. She put two rows of candles on the pie, a row of five and a row of eight. I set the table. We sang "Happy Birthday" to Stephen, who seemed embarrassed and grinned like a kid, before blowing out the candles, all in one noisy go. We ate cherry pie and ice cream. The dogs got pieces of chicken, and for the moment technology was forgotten.

As we talked, Stephen spotted Minnie and Harry nose to nose nuzzling each other. We fell silent and watched until they noticed us and stopped. Carol said that in her mind, Harry was like a rough-and-tumble working-class boy, the kind who might fold a pack of cigarettes in his T-shirt sleeve, but that Minnie was definitely a princess. "But she was a homeless girl," I reminded her. Carol replied, "She must have been kidnapped at birth, because she *is* a princess." Stephen added, "The Lindbergh baby." I can't remember who pointed out that the Lindbergh baby was a boy and that the kidnapping didn't end well.

I asked Carol about the square Hermès box that was still sitting on the table. I thought it might be a present for Stephen. "Oh," she said, "that's the capsule-making machine for Harry's colitis medicine. I brought it over to give you a lesson." I remembered the collection of Hermès boxes in her apartment, and it dawned on me she kept things in them. I opened the box and lifted back sheets of tissue paper, layered as if there really were a present inside. I saw a small white plastic form with what looked like pegs and another matching form with holes in it, sitting on some sort of frame. A page of instructions was neatly folded underneath. Carol opened the plastic bag that had made the rustling noise. Inside were two pouches, each one containing hundreds of little, clear capsule parts, like empty husks, longer ones and shorter ones. I opened one of the pouches, and capsule parts bounced out all over the table and onto the floor. We gathered up as many as we could find, but for weeks I found myself stepping on them, hearing a crunch as they broke into dozens of tiny pieces.

Suddenly, Carol turned to me and said,

"Do you think we could wait and do the lesson another time? I'm really getting tired. I need to go home."

The issue with the doggy cam turned out to be my Wi-Fi. It wasn't good enough to support the thing. In my neighborhood, my provider, my phone company, couldn't offer me anything better, so I had one week to change providers if we were going to be able to watch Harry and Minnie when we went to tea.

I called as soon as Carol and Stephen left to take Harry home that Saturday, and my cable TV company sent someone out on Monday, to my amazement. The technician looked around and informed me he needed to drill a hole through my bedroom wall to my living room so he could install wiring. "It's one hole, straight through, easiest way," he assured me as he made a few quick measurements and knocked on my walls. Why didn't I trust him? "It's no problem," he insisted. He got out a bit that was several feet long and started drilling on the living room side behind my couch. Soon the drill started making a high, whining noise. He turned it off and pulled out the bit. "Hmmm," he said. He went into my bedroom, pulled my bed away from the wall,

135

knelt down, and prepared to drill another hole. Standing over him, I asked, "How do you know the two holes will match up?" His measurements hadn't seemed exact. He looked up at me and said, "They should."

Well, they didn't. The drill made the same high, whining noise again. It had met some sort of resistance — a brick wall, I suspected, since two brownstones had been combined to make the apartments in our building. He pulled his drill out of the wall and once again said, "Hmmmm," but this second *hmmmm* lasted longer than the first one. "I need to go to my truck."

I stood in my living room seething, unable to speak, feeling stupid and helpless as he walked out my front door.

About five minutes later, he came back with a large spool of white cable and a staple gun. "We have to do it this way," he said as he started stapling the white cable to the top of the baseboards along three of the four walls in my bedroom, crawling on his hands and knees out the door, around the hallway, behind a table in my living room and the couch, until finally he stopped, more or less, where I planned to put the new modem. When he was finished connecting everything, my internet worked, but a hill of white dust rose like a little pyramid on the floor under each of the two useless holes he'd made in my walls with no apology.

The next Saturday, I managed, all by myself, to get the doggy cam up and running. My satisfaction was immense, far out of proportion to what I had actually done.

Sunday, October 2, at Tea minus three hours, I dog-proofed my apartment to the best of my ability, just in case Harry and Minnie decided to get into trouble. I emptied my bathroom wastebasket so they couldn't eat batteries or discarded soap. I put the bag of treats I usually leave on my dining table in the kitchen, out of reach at the back of the counter. I stashed my laptop where they couldn't get tangled up in the power cord and dump it on the floor.

For once, Stephen was on time. He had dropped his dog, Teddy, at Ann King's hours earlier, then gone downtown to collect Carol and Harry.

I was in the bathroom when Carol called out from the living room, "Come look at this." Minnie was on the couch tormenting Harry, racing back and forth, nodding her head at him. He crouched and danced around trying to get her to jump down. I grabbed my phone, and this time managed to press the record button instead of the off button. I got more than two minutes of the two of them frolicking and rough-housing. There was no hostility, no tension. It was just two happy dogs playing. I have two minutes and sixteen seconds of video on my phone.

Carol and I were giddy. "Good boy, Harry. Good boy. You need a treat," she said. Never mind that she had told him repeatedly, "No treats." Needless to say, both Harry and Minnie got treats.

We positioned the doggy cam so that its little lens would see most of my living room and turned it on. Images appeared on both of our cell phones. Could it be? I decided to take my charger with me to the tea just in case watching dogs ate up battery.

We set off. Stephen had gone on ahead. Carol was wearing an elegant black jacket, gabardine, vintage I'm sure. She said it was by a French designer but not which one. It had wide, three-quarter-length sleeves, a collar and lapels that were abbreviated so they were trimming, rather than a functional part of the garment's structure. The back was flared, divided into seamed panels. The look was rather Jackie Kennedy Onassis-ish, except that Carol had on crazy shoes Jackie O would never have worn. In the front, they looked like classic Gucci loafers, the kind with a replica of the bit on a horse's bridle across them, but they were actually backless slippers lined with fur. As I faced them, they looked like funny bearded faces.

Me being short, Carol tall, I felt as if I were walking around the block with Big Bird in giant black glasses. She might as well have been covered with yellow feathers, she seemed that flamboyant. As we passed, people looked at us just that extra second or so longer than the normal glance at another pedestrian. I tried to see her with their eyes and noticed that for the first time since I'd known her, her makeup, particularly her lipstick, seemed a little sloppy. She seemed pale. The blouse she wore under her grand jacket had a spot on it. It was work trying to walk slowly enough to stay by her side.

She said she'd been to a birthday dinner for her friend Alan, one of the people I'd met at the party on the roof. "He likes to drink bourbon, so I gave him two antique glasses I brought back from France years ago. He seemed really happy. I'm surprised at how much pleasure I get from giving my things away to my friends. I love seeing their reactions."

She had said almost the same thing to me

before. Was it true? Your treasures are talismans whose magic power is to remind you of a trip or a friend, of a time or a story, of love. What happens to that power when you pass a thing on to someone else, and its meaning changes? What happens when you shed each stand-in for a memory? Do the memories loosen and begin to slip away?

Ann King buzzed us in. "Come up. Come up. You can walk, or the elevator is on the left." She is the kind of Englishwoman who brims with breezy energy. Something about her musical voice is very BBC. It carries and comes from the same place in her chest a singer's does.

Ann King has a sharp wit and a wicked appreciation of both sarcasm and gossip. I would say she's unconventional, but the perfect afternoon tea she prepared for us was exactly the sort Americans imagined that an Englishwoman of a certain age would serve in her snug, tasteful apartment in, say, 1952. On her dining table sat a plate of cucumber sandwiches with the bread crusts cut off, arranged like fingers in concentric circles; next to it a made-from-scratch cake, whipped cream and jam thick between its layers; and if that wasn't enough, a pound cake. Flowered teacups and saucers, plates, linen napkins, and just-polished silver were lined up on a tray.

To complete the picture, there had to be a cat, and, yes, she had one, Samantha, who patrolled the seats of the chairs pulled up to the table, padding between them, flicking her tail back and forth provocatively at Stephen's dog, Teddy, who looked her in the eye and barked. "Tedddeeeey . . ." Stephen chided. "Quiet." Teddy lost interest and flopped down on Ann's white-painted floor in a fluffy, yellow heap. Mary Corliss, who had given the party on the roof, was there. She was listening to Stephen railing about politics. With Donald Trump running against Hillary Clinton, his pronouncements were not exactly arched-pinkie tea talk. It was, after all, a month away from Election Day.

Carol and I asked where there was an electrical outlet, so we could plug in my cell phone charger and fire up the doggy cam. We took turns, with Stephen chiming in, telling the story of what it took to get it to work. This is what the other guests witnessed: two mature (read that *largish*) female backsides turned toward them, Carol's and mine, headless, because we were both rummaging behind the couch trying to plug in the cord as we spoke. The

141

conversation turned to Harry and Minnie as we finally sat down with the phone between us. Yes, they were getting along. No, we didn't anticipate trouble. Look at this video of them playing like wild animals. We just took it, yes, just before we came over here.

When I saw doggy cam video appear on my phone screen, I let out a little, involuntary whoop. Everybody stopped talking. "Yes! Triumph!" I was so excited by my tiny technological achievement; in my mind, it was as if NASA had established communication with the Mars rover.

"What are they doing?" Stephen asked. Carol and I leaned in to look. We kept looking. "Nothing," Carol answered, and looked again. "I don't see them," I said. After everything we'd gone through, nothing.

As Ann and Mary and Stephen talked, about a new play, about movies, about politics again, Carol and I stared, heads bowed, at the palm-size view of my living room, which remained boringly empty. Finally, after servings of cake and compliments and a discussion of notable London tea destinations, I saw movement. "It's Harry."

Again, the conversation stopped. "Well?" Stephen prodded. I squinted and held the phone closer to my face. "I think he's trying to get on the couch." I showed Carol. "He has his front feet on the cushion but can't quite get his back feet up," she said. "But he keeps trying." Pause. Silence. All eyes on us. We continued our play-by-play coverage of Harry's attempted ascent. "Ha! He's almost there. Come on, Harry. You can do it. Go, Puppy Boy." Carol kept cheering him on. He did not appear to hear her. I watched him hop as he tried to fling his left hind leg onto the seat. Carol and I started laughing out loud at his little dance. We stared at the phone and willed him to make it, compelled somehow by a picture about as clear as a sonogram in a doctor's office.

Minutes passed. We were oblivious of the conversation around us . . . and then, "He did it. He did it!" I cried out, interrupting whatever Stephen and Mary were saying. Harry slowly circled a couple of times, stretched himself out, and promptly went to sleep. We watched his back rising and falling, as if watching a dog on a couch breathing were the most fascinating thing in the world. We grinned like idiots.

"Where's Minnie?" Stephen asked. "I don't see her at all." I held the screen maybe three inches from my face. "I'll bet she's on my bed." She never did make an appearance. Harry continued to sleep. Secretly, I hoped they would play. I wanted a little excitement. Not a fight, just something funny. I didn't want to admit that our doggy cam experiment was boring. Successful but boring.

"Now what?" Ann King asked.

"Sleepovers," Carol and I said in unison and giggled.

Carol's favorite picture of herself with Harry, taken circa 2009.

Every occasion an occasion to dress up.

Sir Harry lording it
over the landscape.

Minnie the
Mango Mama.

A chilly day by the Hudson.

Carol's idea wall.

Carol's book of Lake Placid memories.

Harry and Stephen
saying hello.

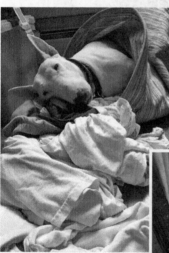

Minnie in her sack.

Minnie playing
hard-to-get.

Harry contemplating theft.

Harry with his bowl and
ball in South Carolina.

Together in bed on
a cold morning.

Harry and Minnie on the
porch in South Carolina.

Carol and the mahjong group in their laurel wreaths.

Carol and the Three Graces.

KATE GODICI

Carol's last walk
with Harry.

Saying goodbye to Harry.
February 26, 2018.

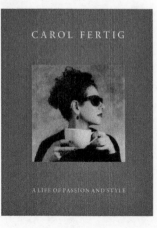

CAROL FERTIG

A LIFE OF PASSION AND STYLE

The program for
Carol's remembrance.

EIGHT:
SLEEPOVERS

Nothing ever goes as planned. For a couple of weeks after the tea, Carol and I got ready for Harry's first sleepover. Her emails ended with exuberant strings of emojis: clapping hands, lips, hearts, dog paw prints. I printed out her three-page directive detailing what he ate and his medications. It included the recipe for his shriveled sweet potato treats with illustrations and a list of names she called him: Harry, Harry Fertig, Puppy Boy, Pupster, PB, Demando Commando, Oompa Loompa, Mr. Loba Loba, and Mister Mister. It ended with the advice that he "loves sleeping on the bed with you." She wrote that he would put his front feet on it, then I would have to boost him the rest of the way by lifting up his back legs. I should "take the opportunity to rub his belly and give him hugs and kisses," and she added, "as much love as possible."

By then it was mid-October. She and Stephen would drive Harry over with his various belongings, food, and medications on Saturday afternoon, or at least that was what was supposed to happen, but Carol took a turn for the worse. For weeks she had been complaining about her stomach. "I think I have a virus," she would say. She went to see her doctors. They told her that it was her cancer closing in. When Stephen called to discuss a Plan B, he used the word "fear" to describe her reaction. Fear was something new, something ominous, but something absent in her emails to me.

In Plan B, Stephen would bring Harry over by himself. The urgency of going ahead with a sleepover was obvious. But then early on the morning of the planned visit, Stephen's dog, Teddy, collapsed with what seemed like the symptoms of a stroke. He had to be taken to a twenty-four-hour emergency veterinary hospital. In fact, he was diagnosed with vestibular disease, a condition of the inner ear that occurs mainly in older dogs. They usually recover from the type Teddy had, but Stephen was a wreck. The sight of Teddy unable to lift his head or control his body made Stephen crazy. He stayed at the hospital all day. So no more Plan B. I was beginning to get rattled.

Plan C. Carol called and booked an appointment at our mutual vet's office to have Harry's toenails cut and for a kind of dog pedicure. Part of the problem with Harry's feet was a condition that caused big dry crusts to form around the edges of his pads. From time to time, the vet had to sand them off with a Dremel tool. Carol phoned to tell me that one of the women in her mah-jongg group, someone with a car, was driving him there and dropping him off along with his overnight bag. It was the first I'd heard of the mah-jongg group. I would soon know much more.

I walked over to get Harry. I knew and dreaded that he came with baggage, all kinds of baggage, in this case probably heavy. What kind of luggage does a dog use for overnights? Harry, I discovered, had what I recognized as an air force helmet bag, slightly shiny, olive green, the kind journalists (me among them) coveted during the Persian Gulf War in 1991. Two zipper pouches on the outside and a roomy central pocket big enough for a helmet. How did Harry manage to get one, and I never did? Inside, I found three kinds of food, his bowl and balls, his various medications, a thick, giraffe-print fleece mat, and the bootie I had loaned Carol. He was limping badly, the crack on the underside of his right foot worse than I'd seen it before. I put the bootie on him and started home. The bootie kept turning around, so the leather sole was on top where it did no good, instead of cushioning his step. I must have stopped ten times to fix it, but it just twisted around again. Each time I bent over and slung his overstuffed helmet bag onto my shoulder, and each time, as I tried to take the bootie off and put it back on again, the bag would slip off my back and fall with a clunk on the sidewalk. And it *was* heavy. Carol had told me several times, "When Harry doesn't want to walk, he just lies down." That's what he did. I'd tug him to his feet. He'd lie down again and give me that slanty, stubborn "I'll show you the whites of my eyes" stare all bull terriers are born knowing. I was getting frantic. People streamed by me on the sidewalk, turning to stare, as if I were abusing this dog.

Suddenly, I realized I had put the bootie on the wrong foot. No wonder he was still limping. How could I have done something so stupid? I would have resisted, too. Even after I put it on correctly, it must have taken forty-five minutes to walk six blocks. When I got him home, I washed his foot, made a proper, padded bandage, and put the bootie on over it. Immediately, he was comfortable. He forgot about limping and suddenly was in the mood to play. I shot cell phone photos and more than three minutes of video of Harry and Minnie tussling, Minnie diving under the coffee table, Harry trying and failing to get at her, the two of them wearing each other out and having a good time. I emailed Carol that I would send the pictures to her, and also that Harry had tried to hump Minnie, but she wasn't in the mood.

The speed of her reply made it obvious that she was at her computer waiting for any shred of news:

From: Carol Fertig
To: Martha Teichner

Dominance. He hasn't humped anyone . . . let alone a girl in a while . . . I think reprimanding is in order. Was his (emoji of flaming candle) out? Nip in bud. "HARRY, NO humping, very bad." Let's see if it happens again. Spray water might do the trick. Also, after a while they get too whipped up. Can't wait to see video.

Back and forth we went, email for email,

149

volley, return. For example, when I un-
packed Harry's things, I didn't see a dog
dish.

At 4:53 P.M., I asked, "Does Harry eat
out of the bowl he plays with, or should I
use one of my dog bowls?"

At 5:02 P.M., she replied, "Not HIS
bowl!!!!!"

At 5:43 P.M., I wrote, "He was just squeak-
ing two balls at once in his mouth. Just as I
got out the cell phone to take his picture,
he dropped them."

At 5:48 P.M., Carol wrote back, "Oh yeah,
that's one of his tricks. Another is 3 balls in
his bowl. Always proud."

And so it went for the next twenty-four
hours, pictures and play-by-play of Harry's
visit. OMGs and emojis (hearts of all kinds,
faces with their tongues sticking out, and
clapping hands) in response.

Feeding Harry his dinner was as difficult
as walking him home from the vet. Carol
had run out of his colitis medication, the
capsules she made herself with the handy-
dandy capsule-making machine she kept in
the Hermès box she'd brought over. She
hadn't felt well enough to make more, and
she hadn't shown me how to use the kit, so
she sent along the full tub of Tylan powder,
I guess hoping I would figure out a way to

get some of it into him. I tried hiding it in ground sirloin. Bad idea. My trick didn't fool him. Harry spit out the meat. The Tylan must have tasted terrible. The powder got on the rest of his food, and he refused to eat. I had to throw it out and make him another dinner.

To me, the perfect Saturday night involves staying home, listening to a book while I cook something nice, my dogs at my feet in the kitchen, followed by a couple of hours on my den couch, watching some old British mystery on television, the dogs on either side of me. That night we did all those things, Minnie and Harry and I, together. It was as if Harry knew the routine already, even which side of the couch was his. I'm sure he did the same things at home with Carol, but I wanted to believe he felt comfortable. For the first time in eight months, since Goose's death, I felt nearly complete, my life almost back in balance. I took pictures of the two dogs on the couch and sent them to Carol.

I have a cord with a hook at each end and a ring in the middle, a kind of coupling, that allows me to walk two dogs on one leash. Around ten-thirty, I hooked them up and took them out together. They poked along beside each other at the same rate of slow, sniffing, stopping. I've always wondered whether dogs communicate telepathically. Harry and Minnie seemed to have agreed on their speed and not to pull in opposite directions. They clearly had the same taste when it came to what was interesting enough to stop and inspect.

Then it was time to go to sleep. Whenever Minnie got up on my bed, she would excavate the sheets and blankets, then roll herself up in them like a cocoon, so tightly that dog walkers have ripped the bedding trying to unwind her to go out. But at night, if I tried to convince her to snuggle in beside me, she would jump off and go to her own bed, on the floor alongside mine. She would paw it as if she wanted to dig herself a hole. When she was satisfied that it was the way she wanted it, she would plop down and wait for me to cover her with blankets, even her head. If she changed positions and found herself uncovered later, she would bark until I woke up and covered her up again. That night, Harry's presence did not disturb her at all or make her jealous. She did what she always did.

Harry, just as Carol predicted he would, wanted to sleep with me. He knew exactly where to go, what to do. He put his front paws on a trunk at the foot of my bed and stared at me with yearning, anticipation — or was it entitlement in his eye? Maybe I'm projecting, but he looked like a small child reaching out to be picked up. I gave him a boost. He climbed onto my duvet, sniffed, circled a couple of times, then made himself comfortable in precisely the spot where I sleep. I took a picture and sent it to Carol. When I got into bed, I had to wake him up. It took my full body weight to move him over a few inches. He settled down with his head on the pillow next to mine, as if he'd been doing it for years. I could hear his breathing and feel his sturdy bull terrier bulk against me.

I hadn't had a dog to sleep with since Goose's death. Goosey and I had worked out our routine the night I got him, when he was a puppy, three months old. I would lie on my side. He would burrow under the covers and nestle in the crook of my legs and snore, his presence a big, soft, warm assurance. I always kept one of his fleece men in the bed. During the night he would find his man and start kneading it with his paws, sucking on one of its arms. This particular night, before turning off the light, I saw the pile of his fleece men on the bench near my bed, each with one extra-long arm, cast aside, no longer needed by anybody but me. Who was this new dog in Goose's place? I started to cry. Was Carol crying, too? I thought about her, alone, with no Harry in *her* bed.

Carol had warned me that Harry often slept till noon. I generally get up between 5:30 and 6:00 A.M. He seemed a bit put out when I roused him to go for a walk. When I emailed Carol a picture of him at 7:35 A.M., awake but still on the bed, she replied, "HARRY got up at 7:35?!?!?"

At noon, I took Harry and Minnie to be blessed. October 4 is the official feast day of St. Francis, patron saint of animals, but churches can be a little loose about scheduling their Blessing of the Animals services on a Sunday around that date, St. Peter's Chelsea included. There must be some sort of rivalry between St. Peter's and the church associated with the General Theological Seminary, a block away, because the seminary held its own Blessing of the Animals a week before the one at St. Peter's. Both are Episcopal churches, although St. Peter's doubles as the nondenominational Chelsea Community Church in order to pay its bills. Both churches were built on land donated by Clement Clarke Moore, who wrote the poem known as " 'Twas the Night Before Christmas." St. Peter's, completed in 1838, is a little like an English country church with Gothic pretensions or the pride of a small village, which Chelsea was in the 1830s.

It always feels like a secret. Once, I suppose, it was considered imposing. It is, after all, built from stone, Manhattan schist, New York City bedrock. You can climb on great hunks of it in Central Park and, if you look hard, catch glimpses of it out the windows of subway cars as you pass through tunnels blasted through it. Manhattan schist held up the city's early skyscrapers. Whoever built St. Peter's Chelsea did it by hand, sorting through piles of stones, tons of stones, laying big ones next to small ones, gray ones next to tan ones, in no particular pattern. The stonework is a wonder. The stones are weathered and dull now. The church seems to be peering out from behind a curtain of leafy old trees and is guarded by a tall wrought-iron fence, as if it's hiding. But its tower gives it away, a stack of stocky squares rising above the treetops, containing a bell and, on each side, a clock, best seen from Ninth Avenue, where you can look up and check whether the visible faces agree on what time it is.

As long as I've lived in the neighborhood (it's hard to believe, more than twenty-five years), St. Peter's Chelsea has been on life support, crumbling, leaking, barely hanging on while its members look for the millions of dollars needed to restore it. Money dribbles in. Repairs never seem to begin or end.

But at Christmas, St. Peter's celebrates by candlelight, its pews garlanded in greenery. Its flaws are hidden and softened for an evening of carols. Shadows dance on its vaulted ceiling obscuring patches in the plaster. The dark woodwork with all its intricately carved points and pinnacles makes the church look theatrical, almost spooky. The organ pipes gleam. Someone from the neighborhood reads the Clement Clarke Moore poem from the pulpit, and for a couple of hours "all is calm, all is bright."

On the rainy, mid-October Sunday of the Blessing of the Animals, all was not calm, and the place seemed dim. Light leaked in through the Tiffany windows, but the church felt chilly, damp. A bucket of dog treats donated by the Barking Zoo, the pet specialty store around the corner, sat at the entrance. The two elderly parishioners handing out programs looked a little ghostly in the gloom as people arrived, mostly with dogs, but a few with cats or birds. The large lizard who had previously attended was absent. There was lots of barking, lots of tail wagging and running around. The small dogs, especially, wriggled and strained and tried to escape their owners' arms instead of sitting quietly.

The blessing at St. Peter's is not one of those extravaganzas where people bring llamas or giraffes. It is an unassuming, do-it-yourself event, although not without intrigue. A member of the choir, Otto, a plumpish occasional actor with a thick brush mustache and a fine tenor voice, who had a hound named Bucky, usually put together the event. Once a police officer brought one of the sniffer dogs who had searched for bodies at Ground Zero. Another year, a woman wrote a poem about dogs. Pet owners from the neighborhood are enlisted to find and present readings about animals. The year Otto talked me into reading, I realized that I had to convince my friend and former dog-walking buddy John to come along, so that he could hold Goose and Minnie while I went up to the lectern. His Australian shepherd, Finny, my dogs' best friend, was still alive then. We all sat together on a tufted velvet cushion, safely shut in behind the kind of latched wooden door often found at the entrance to

157

pews in old churches. We sat there together; that is, until the dogs figured out that they could crawl under our pew into somebody else's pew, where other dogs were waiting.

Eventually, John moved out of the neighborhood, but for today's Blessing of the Animals, Otto had asked him to write lyrics to a song about loving dogs. Otto planned to sing it. John spent weeks working on his song. Finny had died a few months before, so he poured his grief into it. Otto had paired him with a composer, who wanted to go off and write the music on his own, with little regard for John's words and no interest in collaboration. A recipe for trouble. By the time John arrived at my apartment to help me convince Minnie and Harry to walk in the direction of St. Peter's Church, John was no longer speaking to the composer. He was also furious with Otto, although Otto might not have been aware of that. It was John's first time meeting Harry, but even falling in love with him instantly did not improve John's mood, as we nudged and tugged and begged the dogs to follow us. They clearly had zero desire to be blessed. They were cranky. John was cranky. We found ourselves a pew and helped the two dogs up onto the seat. Minnie strained and tried to jump out, over the latched door. It took all my strength to hold on to her. Somebody came along and took her picture squirming and pulling. Harry, mystified by the goings-on, decided he preferred the floor. People ranged up and down the aisles checking out what sorts of animals had shown up, exclaiming how cute they all were.

Finally, the service began. We stood and sang, "All things bright and beautiful, all creatures great and small . . ." and other animal-related hymns. People read. People prayed. The animals were all agitated. When Otto sang his first solo, his hound, Bucky, bayed loudly. The church erupted into prolonged laughter. When Otto sang John's song, I thought it was lovely, the music, the words, Otto's voice, but John muttered under his breath. When people applauded, and Otto introduced John and the composer, John stood and smiled a smile that was closer to a sneer.

At the end of the service, two priests positioned themselves at the back of the church. People wrangled their animals into what was too chaotic to qualify as an actual line up the center aisle, more like a swirl of tails and ears and leashes and arms and coats. This moving mass lurched toward the spot where the priests made the sign of the cross and laid hands on furry foreheads, a benediction the dogs didn't appreciate nearly as much as they did the handful of treats they got from the bucket at the door on their way out. When it was Harry's turn, I asked the priest to give him a special blessing because his owner was dying. He looked at me, then touched Harry's head, closed his eyes, and prayed silently. As we left, John avoided Otto.

Carol's reaction when I emailed her about the Blessing of the Animals was "Glad they were blessed," then a lips emoji and a heart. As much as could be expected from a Jewish atheist.

I delivered Harry and his air force helmet bag back home late Sunday afternoon. Carol's door was unlocked when we got there. She was in bed. Harry was overjoyed to see her and she him. She struggled to get up, slipped her swollen feet into the Gucci slippers she'd worn to tea, and held the edges of her oval table with both hands as she sat down across from me with a gasp. I told her there was no longer any question, I *would* take Harry.

I had been rehearsing how I would say what I told her next. I was worried that she would take it the wrong way. I explained that from the very beginning of the journey we were on together, what we were sharing seemed special to me. I said that after Harry's first visit, I started keeping a diary because I didn't want to forget anything that happened. On Sunday afternoons, on airplanes, in hotel rooms late at night, I wrote, racing to get down the previous week's events before they were overtaken by something else, before I got too far behind. As I did, it began to dawn on me that this was a good story, and I should maybe try to write a book. I had never written a book, so who knew what would happen, I said, but I would only attempt it if I had her permission. If she felt I was in any way intruding, infringing on her right to a private death, I wouldn't do it, I told her, but telling the story would mean that something of who she was would be left behind. She would have to trust that I would get it right.

It was getting dark. Carol hadn't turned on any lights. I stopped talking. She just sat. Then she bent her head, covered her face with her hands, and took long, deep breaths, probably for thirty seconds or so, but it felt like days. Finally, she looked up, straight at me, took another breath, and said quietly, "I would be honored."

I suggested she might contribute to it, too. She said she would and asked if there could be pictures. Having no idea whether publishers, readers, anyone at all, would have any interest, I replied, "I don't see why not."

On Monday, my emails went unanswered. Early Tuesday, I tried again, asking Carol whether she'd heard from Stephen about his dog, Teddy. I said that I'd been trying to reach him but had gotten no reply.

At 9:34 A.M., she wrote:

Teddy is improving!!! But poor STEPHEN put through the ringer so he slept all day yesterday. Am sure he will answer you today. I will write later-just getting up. Yesterday was a bad day for me . . . but saw the Dr. so hopefully improvement on the way. Xc

What did that mean? What kind of bad day? A painful day or a sad day? Or both? What had the doctor given her to make her feel better? Her suffering was a mystery to me, only imagined, hinted at. Unseen but upsetting.

And then at 3:53 P.M., I received this, in a typeface that was supposed to look like hand printing. It was superimposed over Harry's armorial:

162

DEAR MARTHA AND MINNIE,
I HAD SO MUCH FUN WITH YOU
OVER THE WEEKEND. THANK YOU
FOR INVITING ME. I HOPE YOU
WILL INVITE ME BACK. I PROM-
ISE . . . NO HUMPING . . . EVEN
THOUGH I BLAME MINNIE FOR
TEASING ME INTO IT.
BUT, WE HAD SOME FUN!!

YOUR FRIEND,
HARRY FERTIG

At 3:56 P.M., I replied on Minnie's behalf:

Dear Harry,
Minnie is very eager for a return visit.
She's a tease, you know, but she told me
she likes you and hopes you think she's
very beautiful and glamorous . . . she
likes wearing your Aunt Violet's lovely
collar.

Martha

At 3:58 P.M., I got an email with the
subject listed as "From Harry":

I think she's beautiful, but I am not sure
what glamorous means . . . will ask
Carol. Harry Fertig

At 4:04 P.M., I wrote him back:

Harry, my boy, you'll need a Tiffany's charge account to understand . . . Carol will tell you . . .

At 4:06 P.M., Carol helped Harry with his response:

Subject: Re: FROM HARRY

I've been cut off ever since the Petco "incident."

At 4:07 P.M., I wrote:

Unless you're keeping the details secret for fear of prosecution, I'd love to hear THAT story . . . Minnie will just have to get a few film roles to keep her in jewels . . . but she does prefer her men to have a "past."

At 4:13 P.M.:

Subject: Re: FROM HARRY

Nothing racy, just a few treats-(I couldn't help myself they were down low). I've matured since then.

164

At 4:14 P.M., I pressed:

But admit it, the urge still comes over you, right?

At 4:23 P.M.:

Subject: Re: FROM HARRY

I can't say in an email for fear of being hacked. . . . . .

At 4:46 P.M., I admitted:

Confession . . . Even Minnie has entertained notions of shoplifting when confronted with low-hanging treats at the Barking Zoo. With my intervention, she has, in the end, restrained herself.

Her uncle Piggy, however, had a taste for pies at the farmers market. Once, while I was bent over selecting flowers from a bucket of water, he had a glorious two-pie morning, blackberry. By the time I stood up and noticed him gulping them down, a small crowd had gathered to cheer him on. I always had to take extra money with me to pay for his thefts.

Don't tell Minnie I told you about her temptations.

Martha

At 5:17 P.M., from Carol:

HARRY once took a $25 stuffed sheep from Duane Reade . . . I paid for it of course. He shook it wildly all the way home. RESTRICTED!

I sat at my desk in the office staring out my window into the dark laughing and then thought, Oh Carol, how can you hurt so much and bear to be funny.

But it was this email that got me in the gut:

Martha, first of all I want you to know how grateful I am to you that my most precious beast will share the second act of his life with you and Minnie. I couldn't be happier. I can only wish for you that he brings you (and Minnie) as much joy and love as he has brought to me.

I also wanted to thank you for proposing your "project" to me. I am kind of overwhelmed with emotion about the suggestion of it, and also the doing of it.

I look forward to discussing more about your vision of what it should be (mostly structure) so I can begin on my end. I thought that a good way to start for me is to do a kind of "prologue" (just what I have told you about wanting Harry to come to you and the magical way it came for us to meet). If this sounds good to you I'll try to get it on "paper."

Harry is looking forward to his next weekend with his girlfriend.

Xc

Below Carol's signature, her armorial.

The following Saturday, Stephen dropped Harry off and took him home again Sunday. His visit was uneventful, normal. I sent Carol lots of pictures. What she wanted to know was whether Harry had slept with me. I told her he had indeed.

NINE:
THE TIME COMES

The ringing of my phone startled me. It was Stephen, in his car as usual, on the Wednesday after Harry's second sleepover, talking too fast, his voice panicky above the traffic and engine noise.

"I'm really sorry. This is really sudden. Carol isn't feeling well. She's wondering whether you could take Harry for a few days, till Sunday, maybe. I'm headed down there now. I can drop him off tonight."

It was as if I'd been underwater and was suddenly sucked back up to the surface. The call broke my concentration. I was writing a script, immersed in it, coincidentally about dog behavior, and it had to be finished that day. The story was scheduled to air the next Sunday, in four days.

"Uh, what?" I was not quite ready to hear and comprehend.

"I'm sorry," Stephen said again. "Carol says she doesn't feel well enough to take care of Harry right now. She apologizes for asking you to do this so soon after his last visit, with no warning. If you can't, she'll understand, but . . ."

"It's fine. It's fine. It's okay. Please, just bring him over fairly late. I'll need his medications and more of his food with the rest of his stuff." Harry's three kinds of prescription diet. His phenobarbital, sertraline, Tylan, metronidazole, Rimadyl, and trazodone. His giraffe rug, his bowl and balls, and who knows what else would arrive. For his second sleepover, the air force helmet bag had been replaced by a much bigger bag to accommodate everything he'd brought before, plus a few extra toys. I'd laughed when I saw it. Every street vendor in Central America, Africa, the Middle East, and, for that matter, New York City has bags just like it, every farmer hauling produce to market on the back of a donkey. A couple of feet square and a foot or so deep, with a zipper and straps long enough to fit over your shoulder, they're cheap and roomy, coarsely woven out of some sort of cheesy, slightly shiny plastic yarn. They're always plaid. Harry's was red, white, and blue. If plastic had been invented at the time of Christ, Joseph and Mary would have carried their belongings to Bethlehem in one.

I expected the bag to be full to overflowing, just as the one before had been. Unfortunately, something would be missing.

Around the middle of the afternoon, Carol emailed me that as she was packing Harry's things and putting his medications in a pill caddy, she realized she had run out of his phenobarbital. She said she would ask the vet to call in a prescription. She wanted to know the name of a pharmacy near where I lived, since it made no sense to have me traipse all the way down to her local Duane Reade. I gave her the address and phone number of my local Rite Aid and said I would stop there on my way home.

I said that Minnie and I were happy to have Harry. I teased Carol about the street-vendor bag:

From: Martha Teichner
To: Carol Fertig

I hope he doesn't intend to start selling stuff on the street. Then I'll have to get him a storage facility for his wares at Manhattan Mini Storage, and then what will Minnie think?

From: Carol Fertig
To: Martha Teichner

He won't be startin' any street vendor business (he uses that bag to travel incognito. He's a rock star worthy of Miss Minnie. (emoji face wearing sunglasses).

My response:

He's handsome enough to model. . . . I sense that he sings quite a bit, but not sure about guitar cases all over the apartment.

Hers:

He has roadies that store them for him.

Me:

And a rock star bus, no doubt, parked in NJ near Bruce Springsteen's house.

Carol:

Oh yes, they are friends.

Supposedly, when I went to Rite Aid, I would be able to pick up a five-day emergency supply of phenobarbital under the name Harry Fertig. When the pharmacist received a hard copy of Harry's prescription, I could pick up a month's worth.

It was pouring rain when I got off the bus a little after seven, really coming down, cold and windy. I didn't have an umbrella. Stephen had said he would show up at my apartment with Harry at eight. I thought, fine, it's an easy walk. It's just across the street from the bus stop to Rite Aid, and then not even a block home. I'll have plenty of time. Stephen's always late anyway. I won't get too wet.

At Rite Aid, the pharmacist said there had been some sort of mix-up. "I told the vet's office when someone called, I can't, by law, fill Harry's prescription without a hard copy. Phenobarbital is a controlled substance. And anyway, I don't have any in stock and won't be able to get any till at least tomorrow, maybe the day after that."

As I stood at the counter, dripping, swear words were going off in my head like fireworks. I called the vet and asked whether anybody knew of any other pharmacies anywhere in walking distance where I could get some that night. I knew that skipping doses was a bad idea. Harry could go a little crazy without his medication. I called Stephen and told him what was happening.

"I doubt I'll be able to get home by eight."

The vet's office called five different drug-stores before finding one that had phenobarbital in stock. It was maybe a quarter mile walk away, a very wet walk. I stood in line at the pharmacy and waited my turn, only to be told that, yes, the prescription had been called in, but without a hard copy it couldn't be filled. I would have to go to the vet's office, pick it up, and come back. No, it couldn't be faxed. That was the law.

By then it was 7:45 P.M. The vet's office closed at eight. I called and said I was on my way. Rain streaming down my face, in my eyes, I raced to get there in time. I made it with five minutes to spare. One of the receptionists handed me the prescription. I slopped through the rain back to the pharmacy, hoping I'd get waited on before the pharmacist left at 8:30 P.M.

At least five people were ahead of me dropping off or collecting prescriptions. As I stood in line, I caught a glimpse of myself in the mirror on one of those revolving columns displaying reading glasses that always seem to be right next to the pharmacy area. I looked awful. My hair was soaking wet. I had black smudges around my eyes where my mascara had run. My clothes were drenched. I called Stephen again and told him what had happened and

173

that I wouldn't be home for at least half an hour.

"I'll pick you up there," he said. "Right now, I'm ten minutes away. Just look for me out front."

It was nearly nine o'clock when we unloaded Harry and led him inside my apartment. Stephen brought in Harry's street-vendor bag, which was fuller than ever. Harry and Minnie immediately started playing. I sent Carol a picture of the two of them lying side by side staring at me, imploring me to feed them.

She wrote, "They know from whence their bread is buttered." I wrote, "And their chicken is shredded, and their sweet potatoes roasted."

Harry refused to sleep with me that night. He slept in the living room on an upholstered chaise longue near the door to the garden. The following day my au pair showed me a pair of what had been tassel loafers, except the tassels were gone, chewed nubs all that were left where they'd been. "Harry chewed up my new shoes." My au pair was angry.

Carol emailed to ask, "How goes it on 22nd St.?" I told her about the shoes, explaining how my au pair "tends to creep in very late, take them off, and leave them by the dining table so he won't make noise on the hardwood floors. . . . Maybe Harry is feeling insecure and confused."

Carol replied:

OMG, I am mortified about the shoes!!!!!! He never does stuff like that. He MUST be feeling insecure and confused. Please tell [him] to email with cost of shoes, and I will pay him. . . . I hope he has it in him not to hold it against HARRY. I think he is going through a difficult time. I am saddened about this. . . .

Then I did a little checking and discovered the truth.

From: Martha Teichner
To: Carol Fertig

[He] said it was Harry who ate the tassels off his shoes, but when I asked him when he discovered the damage, he said, "Yesterday morning." That means it couldn't have been Harry. He wasn't here to do any damage. It had to have been Minnie. Please forgive us. . . . I hope Harry accepts my apology. . . . Minnie likes eating bra clasps, so I guess shoe tassels are equally appealing. Minnie is sneaky. She wants you to think she's very, very good, but isn't always. . . .

From: Carol Fertig
To: Martha Teichner

That Minnie! She has a double life. I hope she doesn't lead HARRY down the road to ruin!! Xc

A few days later, on Saturday, I was at work when Stephen called, apologetic to be delivering more bad news. "I'm so sorry this seems to be happening sooner than anticipated. Carol says she feels that she can't take care of Harry properly anymore, and maybe she should turn him over to you now." It was always Stephen who called, never Carol. I could only guess that she was too sick to talk, or maybe that she couldn't bring herself to say out loud, to say to me, that her cancer was overtaking her.

I was busy. My story had to get done for air the next day. No, this couldn't be happening, not yet. I felt a little faint. I felt as if I were falling. I could hear Stephen breathing into the phone. Seconds passed before I could answer.

"No, it's fine." I replayed in my head what Carol had said about hanging on to Harry till the very end and about lying on the floor with him as her way of following doctor's orders to do one joyful thing a day. I couldn't imagine what it took to make the decision. She knew that giving up Harry was giving up on Life, and then she would get on with the business of dying.

Stephen said, "She told me she's trying to see it as if Harry's going off to college, leaving her an empty nester."

Humor takes courage, I thought.

TEN:
RED JELL-O AND HALLOWEEN

"She doesn't have to make that decision now," I said. "It doesn't have to be final." Stephen and I were in his car the next day, driving to Carol's. "No, I know," he replied, "but she said it was final. She's really worried that she can't take care of him." I suggested the obvious. "We could take Harry to visit her. She could have the pleasure of being with her dog without worrying about feeding him or taking him out." Stephen nodded. "Maybe we can convince her. I hope so." I did, too.

When we walked into Carol's building, we found ourselves wading into a sea of little kids in costume carrying buckets of candy and plates of cupcakes, darting this way and that, changing direction like startled fish, their moms and dads with plastic swords in hand or a discarded tiara, trying to keep track of them. We got in the elevator with a swarm of superheroes and princesses. The

178

building was having its annual Halloween party.

Carol's door was unlocked. She was propped up in bed, chalky gray, her skin waxy, her hair messy, stuck flat against the back of her head where she'd been leaning back against her pillows. She wasn't wearing makeup, but she was wearing a beautiful black-and-white silk kimono. Fashion, always fashion, I thought.

"I'm tired *all* the time," she said, "just exhausted. My stomach bothers me. Look in the refrigerator. People have brought me a regular chicken coop full of rotisserie chickens. I can't even look at them."

She had asked Stephen to buy her red Jell-O. He had hunted all over his neighborhood. He couldn't find the glistening, ruby-red kind kids take in their school lunches or hospitals put on meal trays. The best he could do was something reddish that said "healthy" and "vegan" on the label. He pulled an individual serving cup off one of the two six-packs of the stuff he had brought and handed it to Carol along with a spoon. Carol peered at it. She didn't have her glasses on, so she held it three inches from her nose and turned it over, scowling at the color. She tried it, stared at Stephen, then handed the spoon and the cup back to him.

"It's disgusting," she announced.

Stephen stared back and then finished it off. "What's wrong with it?" he asked, pretending to be put out.

"*Real* Jell-O is totally artificial, artificial flavor, artificial color, and it's loaded with sugar," she said, fully aware of what she was saying, her voice full of mock sarcasm. "My favorite is cherry. This isn't cherry. I don't know what it is." Carol was starting to perk up. She and Stephen were enjoying this game.

He continued, "So if it isn't bad for you, you don't like it. . . ."

"No." She grinned. "If it isn't bad, it isn't good."

Stephen changed the subject. "What's *that*?" He pointed to what looked like a cross between the top half of an armchair and the abominable snowman parked on a chest of drawers. It was covered in some sort of thick, scraggly white shag. "That's bizarre," I said.

She sighed. "Isn't it. . . ." We all considered its ugliness. "A friend of mine gave it to me thinking I could use it to sit up in bed." She regarded it with the same contempt she had shown the vegan Jell-O. "I like soft pillows. I can arrange them." She turned and punched her pillows. "I guess I'll have to get it out whenever she comes over."

The apartment door opened. A cheery voice called out hello. Carol smiled. "It's Lissa and my young friend."

I would come to know Lissa Hussian well in the next few weeks. Tall, slim, young looking but probably fortyish, she approached Carol's bedside wearing a black dress, black tights, big black sunglasses, a blond wig styled in a bob, spike heels, and a mink wrap. She was supposed to be Anna Wintour, the editor of *Vogue.*

She put her arms around the shoulders of her six-year-old daughter, Annabelle, who was dressed up in a Rockettes costume, the red toy-soldier suit slightly large. Her plumed hat was tilted sassily. A teasing comma of chin-length brown hair framed her jawline below it. She wore sparkly red knee-high boots. She was sucking on a lollipop, holding the handles of a paper bag filled with trick-or-treat candy, looking shy. Her eyes were serious. The flirtiness of her outfit exaggerated the innocent, childlike roundness of her face. The two of them lived in the building and had been to the Halloween party.

Carol beamed and asked Annabelle questions about the party and school.

Stephen had a funny look in his eye, a

combination of malice and mischief as he glanced first at Carol, then at Annabelle. "Do you like Jell-O?" he asked. She nodded a cautious yes. He tore off another little cup from the six-pack and handed it to her. Lissa got her a spoon. She took a bite and another and then ate the whole container. Stephen watched, a grin slowly stretching across his face so wide that the twirled ends of his mustache turned up. "Good?" he asked. She smiled and nodded again. He gave Carol a look of exaggerated triumph. "Why don't you take these home," he said, handing over the rest of the Jell-O to Annabelle. Carol ignored him.

"Go get the picture." Carol motioned to Lissa, who retrieved a framed photograph and brought it over to show me.

Carol, Lissa, and four other women stood side by side, smiling at the camera. At first I couldn't quite make out what was going on in the photo. They were all wearing nightgown-like, white garments, cord wrapped around their waists two or three times, spray-painted gold laurel wreaths on their heads. Bigger and older than the others in the photo, wearing her huge black glasses, Carol stood out.

"Togas?" I asked. Carol explained, "Togas, yes. Our mah-jongg group. We don't really know how to play mah-jongg very well, so we sometimes dress up or go shopping. We've been known to go to the cosmetic department at Duane Reade and look at nail polish colors, for instance."

"Carol made the laurel wreaths," Lissa said.

"I used to belong to a book club that prided itself on not reading the books. We just sat around and talked," I said. "Like that?"

"Exactly." Carol laughed.

The mah-jongg group had become much more than a few friends pretending to play mah-jongg, putting on costumes, or going on giggly girls' outings with Carol as ringleader, instigator. Lissa, Kate, and Cecilia were particularly close to Carol. Once, they were her posse, her eager acolytes, happy to join in the little adventures she concocted, to laugh and be silly and revert to girl talk. Mothers, wives, or ex-wives, professionals, women with complicated lives, they all gladly fell under Carol's slightly madcap spell, which gave them the comic relief and camaraderie they needed. As Carol got sicker, they turned into her women's brigade, her support team. They divided up responsibilities. Cecilia got over her fear of dogs and took care of Harry. Kate cleaned, did Carol's laundry, changed her sheets, assisted with her legal affairs, badgered the 9/11 Victims Compensation Fund about her claim. Lissa looked after Carol herself, spending time with her, going with her to doctors' visits, organizing hospice care. The three of them got her to eat, ran errands for her, made her laugh, listened. They were goddesses in the picture and for real. I gave them a name, the Three Graces.

When Lissa took Annabelle home, with her bag of Halloween candy and the vegan Jell-O, Carol groaned as she pulled herself up to a sitting position. It was as if the show was over, and she could stop acting. She swung her legs slowly to the floor and struggled to stand. Her feet were swollen, even more swollen than the last time I'd been to see her. Her Gucci loafer slippers were parked by her toes, but she shuffled barefoot across the room, and I saw how slowly she was moving. At her kitchen counter, she poured glasses of water for the three of us. Her fingers were shakier than the last time I'd seen her. The glasses wobbled dangerously. Stephen took them from her and we sat down at the table.

As we drank our water, the conversation turned to Harry. Carol told me that Stephen had driven her to the breeder's home in New Jersey eleven years before, during the summer of 2005, to pick out a puppy. She originally selected the one she thought was the handsomest, but was informed he wasn't for sale. He was "show quality, not pet quality," she said, so she chose Harry instead. Not long after getting him home, she went on, she sent Stephen a picture of herself with Harry. "You know what Stephen said? 'He's got your eyes.' " We all laughed. They looked at each other, remembering.

Eventually, Carol braced her palms against the tabletop, support she needed all the time now, I realized, and heaved herself out of her chair. She was breathing heavily and coughing when she reached her kitchen counter, a few feet away, and rested her elbows on it. "I'm getting really tired. This is the rest of Harry's medicine." She reached out an arm and raked at least a dozen pill bottles toward her. So many. "Sertraline and trazodone for his anxiety disorders, Rimadyl for arthritis. You know all that. Metronidazole for diarrhea, heartworm medication, flea-and-tick-prevention tablets, some old antibiotics." She gathered up eardrops and ointments and allergy shampoos and dog toenail clippers and then pushed an orange-and-brown Hermès box toward me. The

185

capsule-making kit. How many times had she said she would give me a lesson? She was handing it over to me along with the bag of capsule shells and tubs of Tylan powder. I understood there would be no lesson.

Carol made her way across the room, coughing some more, her pain visible in every step. She opened a closet and strained to pick up two overflowing shopping bags. Stephen rushed over to her. "I can do that." He took the bags and set them on the table. "Go get in bed." She didn't. Carol wanted to show me Harry's wardrobe.

Out of the bags, she pulled a shiny black patent-leather raincoat and then a red plaid fleece-lined winter jacket with black and silver biker patches stitched on all over it: HARLEY-DAVIDSON, THE SONS OF ANARCHY, ORIGINAL UNHOLY ONES, LIVE TO RIDE. There were skulls and skeletons, a Maltese cross, and a strange tan patch with two words in Greek letters. To go with the jacket, he had a turtleneck sweater with a white skull and crossbones knitted into it. Next, Carol produced a black down-filled varsity jacket lined in red, covered with pins. For example: DAVID BOWIE IS TURNING US ALL INTO VOYEURS, I DID IT, C'EST LA VIE, I ♥ BEAUTY, RAMONES, CHER IS MY MOM,

I'M WITH STUPID, I HAVE SEEN THE FU-
TURE, JUST SAY NO TO DRUGS. One had a
picture of a skateboarder on it, another the
British flag. There was an owl pin, a duck-
ling, and a Bakelite bull terrier head that
looked like Harry's. A walking social statement, that dog. "It's a good thing he doesn't
vent on the internet," I said. Carol smiled. I
smiled. I admired the cleverness of the
clothes, her playfulness, her creativity. I
commented on what a fashionable fellow
Harry was, very cool. I didn't say that I
found her composure excruciating to wit-
ness. I didn't ask how she could bear this
show-and-tell without breaking down. These
clothes represented how much she loved
him. Did she feel a physical ache? Knowing
this moment was coming, had she cried . . .
alone? Or had someone been there to see
her through her anguish?

Last, she laid out a white plush unicorn
costume, with pink ears, a lavender satin
horn, and a purplish mane and tail. "Lissa
and Annabelle bought this for Harry to wear
to the Halloween party. Normally, I make
his costume, but not this year." She sighed.
"He didn't get to wear it."

Stephen said, "Carol won the Halloween
costume contest for dogs downtown so
many times, she was told she wouldn't be

allowed to win anymore."

We heard a noise, a splat against the windows. We looked out into the darkness and saw that it was raining, hard, as if the wind were flinging buckets of water against the glass. Time to leave. Stephen stuffed Harry's clothes back in the shopping bags as well as his medicines and the capsule kit.

"Carol, we can bring Harry to visit you." I had to say it. "You can enjoy him without having to worry about anything. He's fine with going back and forth. He's already done it a lot. You need him."

She looked at me for a good five seconds, then whispered, "No. It would break my heart."

ELEVEN:
A GIFT FOR FRIENDSHIP

Stephen and I looked at each other but didn't speak when we left Carol's apartment. We said nothing as we waited for the elevator, heard it ding, got in. Stephen can't help himself. He talks. He fills silences, but here he was . . . silent. We crossed the lobby. At the side entrance, all he said was "You should stay here. I'll get the car and come back." I handed him my umbrella.

"It would break my heart. It would break my heart." Carol's words repeated in my mind as the automatic doors opened and closed, opened and closed, whenever someone came into the building or left or if I stepped too close to them trying to see whether Stephen had pulled up outside with his car, hoping it would be soon. Each time the doors opened, wind rushed in and rain splattered me as I waited with the various bags of Harry's things. Every blast was an affront, an annoyance, a pang, and made me impatient. It had turned cold. We had parked four or five long blocks away. I knew the neighborhood was a crazy puzzle of one-way streets. To reach the side door of Carol's building, Stephen's car would have to be searched at one of the security checkpoints that had been erected at either end of the New York Stock Exchange after 9/11. I understood why he seemed to be taking forever, not why I was so bothered.

How many people would do for another person what Stephen did for Carol? He went to visit her practically every day. He drove her and Harry to my place and back. He worried. He obsessed. He brought her movies and sat with her half the night watching them when she was in pain or couldn't sleep, brought her food she said she wanted but didn't eat. And what about Lissa? I had seen the delight on Carol's face when Lissa arrived with Annabelle. "My little friend," Carol called the shy girl in her Rockettes costume.

I felt cheated that I had only known Carol for three months. I was jealous of all the people who had been her friends for decades. I remembered the night she'd brought Harry over, that I said, "I wish I'd known you for twenty years." She replied, "Me too." I felt cheated that there would be no more years. But we *were* friends, close friends there and then, and I was grateful.

As I think back, when I was in college and then in my twenties, making friends was like the days getting longer in the spring. No matter how busy I was, there was always more time to talk, time enough to cut through the social niceties, time enough to know someone. I consider the friends I made then some of my closest friends still. They're the planets in my personal solar system. I know myself by their presence in my being. I feel their gravitational pull, even though I usually only hear their voices now, hollow and far away, on birthday calls. I see their faces in the gallery of mental snapshots I visit, aware that the pictures in my mind are out-of-date.

People get busy. Possibility does battle with routine, and routine wins. Life steals our time. Our days get shorter, our worlds smaller, the way in harder.

I've moved nine times since college, from Cambridge, Massachusetts, to Grand Rapids, Michigan; from Grand Rapids to Miami; from Miami to Chicago; from Chicago to Atlanta; Atlanta to London; London to Dallas; Dallas to Johannesburg; Johannesburg back to London; three years here, four or five years there, until the last move,

from London to New York, where I've been
for more than twenty-five years. But I travel.
It's the nature of my work. During a dozen
years as a foreign correspondent, I was often
away from home for months, usually covering wars. For journalists in a war, the
language of friendship is storytelling. They
tell stories at night in the bar of a press hotel
or crammed together in the back of a truck
crossing a desert. When people with little in
common except for their proximity and
their profession have nobody but each
other, that's what they do. In a war zone,
friendships are intense, ignited by danger
into a bright, hot light. The photographer
or fixer next to you when you're shot at is
your friend in a way no one else can be.
Seeing the same horrors, feeling the same
fear, you know what you've shared and
don't have to talk about it. It's easy to fall
in love or think you have. For a time, no
other people exist. No other place seems
real. And then it's time to leave. You say
goodbye till the next time or maybe forever.
That's it. No more bright light. Like turning off a switch. You go home. Supermarkets
and movies and flowers in parks and people
hurrying to work are an alternative universe,
hard to comprehend, unnatural, a little
colorless. Maybe you're lucky and have a

few friends or family members who understand. Or maybe there just isn't enough
time until the next war or the next transfer
to find a hole in the loneliness that can sur-
round you like fog.

You snatch at good times, at opportunities
to make new friends, because of all the
cancellations: quick calls on the way to the
airport to say, "Sorry, I won't be able to go
to dinner after all" or "I know we had a
date, but I'm going to Iraq" . . . or Bolivia
or Lithuania or Bosnia, East Germany, the
West Bank, Libya, Northern Ireland, et cetera, et cetera, fill in the blank. Those cancellations all felt like failure, like loss to me,
but those destinations felt like history, and
journalists are, after all, in the history business. I knew what getting into that business
meant, the price of admission, the risks. I
didn't know how high the cost would be. I
wanted a husband and children, lots of
friends, a social life, but did I want them
enough to give up the opportunity to wit-
ness history and write about it? After decades of asking myself that question, I still
haven't been able to answer it. I learned to
live with loneliness and treasured my friends
and my momentary escapes into normalcy.
They felt like coming up for air.

A few months out of college I adopted a

big, shaggy shelter dog, who looked as if he were impersonating a lion. No one at the shelter knew his name. People asked me, "What are you going to call that beast?" I called him Beast. He moved with me from Cambridge to Grand Rapids to Miami to Chicago to Atlanta. If loneliness, like poison, can have an antidote, that's what Beast was. I found people to walk him and take care of him when I was out of town, usually just a few days at a time at that stage of my career. He made demands. He was tricky and sly and occasionally diabolical. I loved him desperately and had him for ten years. He died a few months before I was transferred from Atlanta to London. I can say it now, but couldn't then. His timing was perfect. He would have had to spend six months in quarantine before being allowed to live in the UK, and based in London, I was away so much, I couldn't possibly have a dog, or so I thought. But the pain of losing Beast ached on and on. The loneliness came back.

For seven years, I tried not to forget how it felt to touch him and dreamed of having another dog. Then, I was posted to South Africa. I worked late most nights, given the six-hour time difference between Johannesburg and CBS News headquarters in New York but traveled little. I rented a house with a nice, big garden and a shaded patio and had a live-in housekeeper.

I found myself paging to the back of the Sunday newspaper almost every week and allowing myself a glance at the classifieds, under "Pets." Just looking, I told myself, until I spotted an advertisement for bull terrier puppies and remembered Petrus, the bull terrier at the winery, sitting on my feet. The puppies were squirming around in a big box. I picked the naughty one who climbed over all his brothers and sisters to see what was going on. His registered name was Borrible Napoléon Bone, but I didn't want him getting any ideas about taking after that other Napoléon. It might be better to call him something else. My vet asked, "What are you going to name that racing pig?" Bull terriers do look a little like pigs, so I named him Piggy. I conveniently overlooked the question of what would happen to him when my three-year assignment in South Africa ended and I was sent back to London. Like Beast, he was tricky and sly and diabolical, which is exactly what I loved about him, from the moment he began to wreak havoc in my household. It occurred to me that if he were a boyfriend, he'd be bad news, exactly the kind of man to avoid.

■ ■ ■ ■

So why do we fall in love with animals instantly and forgive them their trespasses but find it so much harder to make human friends? I took it for granted that that's just how it was, until that Saturday I went to the farmers market with Minnie, and friendship took me by surprise.

The sliding doors opened suddenly, and there was Stephen, stamping rain off his shoes, shaking water off the umbrella I had loaned him for the dash to his car. He's the kind of person who creates commotion wherever he goes. "At the checkpoint, when the dogs smell Teddy's cushions in the back, they get confused and wag their tails. That's a signal to the officers that they've found something suspicious. My whole car got searched." We picked up Harry's belongings and ran through the rain.

The windshield wipers were on their fastest speed, urgent and loud in the dark car, *whap, whap, whap.* Stephen had trouble seeing where he was going, it was raining so hard. For a while, we didn't talk. Finally I said, "Carol has a real gift for friendship, I think."

"She does. We've had our fights. There have been times when we haven't spoken for months, but in the end, we always make up. It's like that with everybody she knows. My ex-boyfriend, Paul . . . Paul Number One. I had two boyfriends named Paul. Remember when you used to see me walking three goldens at Chelsea Piers? Two of them were his. Anyway, he had a huge falling-out with Carol. They were going to buy a fancy stationery company together. She blamed him when the deal fell through and felt deeply hurt. They didn't speak, but now they're friends again."

I asked Stephen whether he'd known either of Carol's husbands. "No, I didn't even know she was married twice."

"That's what she told me."

"In one of her earlier apartments, she had a very large painting the first one did, his take on rococo style, voluptuous bodies . . . but refined." Stephen paused to make a turn. "You know, Fertig is her married name. I don't even know her maiden name." Another pause. "I've known her for . . . maybe . . . thirty years. In that whole time, I don't recall her ever being in a relationship."

"What about her family?"

"She has a brother, but they're estranged.

He has a son she got to know when he was at NYU. She's crazy about him. She had a really complicated relationship with her parents. Her father was an alcoholic. Her mother was . . . strange. Both dead. She told me recently that she was sexually abused by her mother's shrink when she was fifteen. She said she repressed what happened for years and finally remembered it . . . maybe that's had an effect on her ability to sustain relationships . . . although she has tons of friends."

By the time we reached my street, the rain had stopped. Stephen asked to come in and say hello to Harry, who jumped all over him and wagged his tail wildly. He picked up his bowl and ball but dropped them with a clunk when he spotted the shopping bags. He plunged his head in the one filled with his jackets, snuffling loudly. I wondered whether he smelled Carol. I took his picture, head in bag, and emailed it to her.

The next morning, I sent a new picture and another the day after that. I'd been sending her pictures or videos since the first time Harry had come for a sleepover. She emailed back, asking whether I thought he was sad. "I don't know." I said I thought he liked being with Minnie and me but hadn't quite figured out what was expected of him.

"I'm sure he misses you, though." Carol replied, "Maybe I am projecting."

I realized that many of the pictures I'd sent showed Harry lying down or looking away, not so many videos of the two dogs playing. I found another one, a picture of Harry on his giraffe-print rug looking straight into the camera, his bowl at his feet, and forwarded it. The email I got a few minutes later had no words, only a large heart.

I replied, "A big red heart, like the red, lipstick kisses the dogs get before I leave for work. They don't show up on Harry as much as on Minnie, but he gets them."

"I'm counting on it!" Carol followed her exclamation point with an emoji lipstick kiss. The next morning, I sent her pictures of the dogs with red kisses on their foreheads.

I began to worry. Was Harry sad? Did Carol see in the pictures something I didn't recognize because I hadn't known Harry long? I felt an obligation to be candid, so I emailed her:

Last night I couldn't find him. Finally, I noticed one of my dining chairs tipped back, my dog-walking jacket hanging on it. I looked and discovered Harry trapped

with his head stuck in my pocket, undoubt-
edly after treat crumbs. I do think he may
be sad. I try to get him to play with his
bowl and his balls, but he'll only do it for a
minute. . . . I cuddle him and talk to him,
and he seems to like that, but I think he
misses you. . . . He likes sitting with me
on the couch in the den. I just can't get
him to play much. He likes being a bathroom guard in the morning and conks out
on the bath mat, when he gets tired of licking my legs and feet. I hope he's ok. He
just isn't being demonstrably silly.

I shouldn't have said anything. Carol was
alarmed.

From: Carol Fertig
To: Martha Teichner

Oh God Martha I feel awful. If it keeps
up perhaps Dr. Farber could put in a
few wise words. The only thing I can
recommend is lots of love — physical
and talking etc. I do think some of this
is to be expected. Does he play with
Minnie at all? Please keep me posted.
Xc.

I felt awful, too. I had upset Carol. I didn't
know what was going on with Harry. Was

he pining for her? Did he miss his home? It was Thursday night, November 3. I was unbelievably busy, preoccupied, trying to finish a story summing up the entire presidential campaign for that Sunday's show, the Sunday before the 2016 election. *And* I had to fly to Charlottesville, Virginia, that Saturday to shoot a different story. That meant I would be working a succession of fifteen-hour days. *And* I was worried about Harry. My tongue felt too big for my mouth. I was clenching my teeth.

I got home that night around nine. It was as if the dogs knew Carol and I were turning ourselves inside out. Immediately they started one of their wild romps. Minnie jumped on the couch. Harry snatched one of the pillows. Minnie dashed under the dining table. Harry ran after her. A few minutes later, Harry picked up his bowl and balls and jiggled them enthusiastically. Minnie bowed and growled and pretended she wanted to steal the bowl from him, so that he would chase her. Somehow, I didn't screw up the video. How could that be? I was thrilled and relieved and suddenly relaxed. I emailed the videos to Carol. In the heading, under "Subject," I wrote, "I shouldn't have worried."

At 3:44 A.M. on Friday, Carol answered,

"thank you thank you thank you."
I saw her reply when I got up and realized she wasn't sleeping.

TWELVE:
JOYRIDE

Stephen was going to take Carol out for what he called a "joyride," and I was invited to come along. The Three Graces had signed her up for Hospice Home Care. A wheelchair and walker were delivered to her apartment. She asked Stephen to hide them, so she and her visitors could pretend they weren't there, but Sunday, November 13, was supposed to be a beautiful, unseasonably warm day, perfect for rolling around outside in the warm sunlight. "Bring Teddy," she told Stephen. We tried to convince her to let us bring Harry, too, but she was adamant. "Too painful," she said. She instructed me to come with a tape recorder and microphone, so she could talk about her life and Harry's for the book. She hadn't felt well enough to do any writing.

The plan was that Stephen would pick me up between 1:15 and 1:30 P.M. Fat chance, I thought. At 1:11 P.M., I got a message, as

203

I expected I might, that he was running behind. A few minutes later, he texted again: "EMERGENCY. Phone me."

"Carol fell trying to take a shower," he said. "Lissa found her." Carol was in pain and wanted Stephen to come quickly. He was about to leave and was talking too fast, the usual sign that he was upset. I offered to get in a cab and join him at Carol's, but he said no, he'd let me know when he knew what was going to happen.

I sat staring at my cell phone, Harry cuddling on one side of me, Minnie on the other, oblivious. I felt panicky, but also helpless and let down, because I'd been looking forward to recording Carol's stories, and now it wouldn't happen. I'd been picturing her joyride in my mind. What right did I have to be disappointed when the only real concern was Carol's condition? Why was I upset at having to sit out the crisis at home? I wanted to do what friends do, what I so rarely could do: be there. I'm a person who makes her living peering in from outside. For once, I wanted to be inside, but I had to be honest with myself, my presence wasn't the issue. This wasn't about what I wanted. It was about what Carol needed.

I walked around, trying to figure out what to do with myself. The dogs shifted their positions when I got up. Minnie had her head on the pillows at one end of the couch. Harry rested his head on Minnie's haunch. I took a picture of them there, sleeping, as if they'd been together all their lives.

That picture was one more acknowledgment that Harry had moved in, that he wasn't just visiting. I'd printed out a couple of photos on a copy machine, one of Harry by himself, the other of Harry with Minnie, and taped them to my office door, which is covered with pictures of bull terriers. Target dogs, cartoon bull terriers on *New Yorker* magazine covers, Piggy, Goose, Minnie. I'd taken Harry to the farmers market for the first time. I'd opened the orange Hermès box, unfolded the tissue paper, gotten out the capsule maker, and, after much trial and error, made twenty-four capsules for Harry. One last thing: I'd needed to change the password on my computer. I thought of one with an *H* in it for "Harry," then wondered whether I had the right to take possession. He was part of my life, but as long as Carol was alive, I told myself, he would not truly be mine. We were still sharing him in our hearts if not in fact. And then I told myself, It's just a password.

At 3:20 P.M., I emailed Stephen: "Any news?" At 3:38 P.M., he replied, "We are at the hospital. They are doing an EKG. Nothing new to report yet. I will keep you informed." As it turned out, instead of taking Carol for a joyride in the wheelchair, Stephen and Lissa struggled to lift her into it as she groaned in pain. They wheeled her through the lobby, hauled her up into Stephen's car, and drove to NYU Langone Hospital.

The details dribbled out, one phone call at a time. Carol had broken several bones in her back, her vertebrae weakened by the radiation she'd undergone to shrink the tumor on her spine. She was diagnosed with pneumonia, and the cancer had reached her lungs, which explained the cough that wouldn't go away. Her white blood cell count had gone from 15 to 19.8 in two weeks, another bad sign, I assumed. She was on two different kinds of intravenous antibiotics.

Stephen let me know when he was about to go home to feed Teddy and take him out. In the morning, he called me again. "Lissa stayed. She told me this little group came in to report to Carol the results of the tests they did. The guy in charge was an intern . . . young, kind of cocky." Stephen was indignant. "He announces that she needs major surgery, immediately, to fix the spine fractures and then two months of intense rehab. Carol looked at him like he was crazy and said, 'I won't be alive in two months. Didn't you read my history?' Lissa couldn't believe a doctor would say that."

I couldn't believe it either. The cruelty of his incompetence was stunning. I said to Stephen, "I blame myself. If I hadn't been planning to come over with the recorder, Carol wouldn't have taken a shower and fallen." He interrupted, "No, I was mistaken. She didn't fall taking a shower. She was trying to go to the toilet. You had nothing to do with it." I felt a little better.

It was the second time she'd fallen. Stephen told me about how the first time she hadn't been able to get up until someone arrived to help her. He said that in the two weeks since I'd seen her, she'd deteriorated noticeably. One night she called and asked him to come and cook a bacon omelet for her and to bring Teddy. He bought the eggs and the bacon and drove downtown, but when he arrived, he found her in bed, retching into a bowl. "I've never seen her that way. She couldn't even speak. I stayed till eleven-thirty, because I couldn't leave. She was pitiful. She has some new cough medicine, something with codeine in it. She took it and finally fell asleep. She hadn't slept at all the night before."

Then Stephen told me about Bruno. I had just about forgotten about Bruno, Carol's twenty-two-year-old cat. "Not this past Friday, a week ago, she called and told me that Bruno wouldn't stop crying. He wasn't keeping himself clean. He wasn't eating. On Saturday, Lissa took him to the vet. Kidney failure." Lissa called Carol, who told her to go ahead and have him put down. That was that.

Stephen said that when he visited Carol on Monday, she'd seemed detached, unemotional about Bruno. "When I got there, all Bruno's things were gone, his bowls, his food, everything. Lissa probably." I told him that Carol had always seemed unconcerned about what would happen to Bruno, almost as if she knew the situation would resolve itself. "I asked her about him several times. She would shrug or change the subject."

Stephen sighed. "Harry is another story."

That night, I emailed Carol a picture of Harry in my bed and the one of Harry and Minnie sleeping on the couch. In the subject box, I wrote, "H and M and I are worried about you." A little after midnight she wrote back that in the hospital, she couldn't open pictures and that she was worried, too.

THIRTEEN:
CATCH-22

Thank you, Joseph Heller, for giving the English language a name for idiotic, illogical, senseless bureaucratic impossibilities.

Carol was brought to the emergency room at NYU Langone Hospital that Sunday. Finally, after hours of tests, she was taken to a room. You might assume that being transferred from a gurney to an actual bed meant she had been admitted to the hospital. Wrong. She was still, technically, an emergency room patient. On Monday, she was told that since she had decided against treatment for the broken bones in her back, she could no longer remain in this jurisdictional limbo. She would *not* be admitted. She had to leave. She was in such pain she couldn't stand up. She had pneumonia and was dying of cancer, *but,* according to Medicare regulations, the hospital was not *allowed* to admit her. Rules were rules. She was free to go home. Of course, she couldn't go home without twenty-four-hour care, *but,* Medicare requirements again, she didn't qualify. She could pay out of her own pocket. The only problem, she didn't have any money because she couldn't work.

Carol had wanted home hospice services thinking caregivers would come to her apartment, but discovered she wasn't considered close enough to death. On that Sunday afternoon, after her fall, Lissa and Stephen tried to call her oncologist . . . and tried . . . and tried. When they finally reached him, he said to take her to NYU Langone Hospital rather than the closest emergency room since he was on staff there and could look after her. On Monday, Lissa and Stephen both tried to call him again. No reply.

Lissa and another of the Three Graces, Kate, confronted the hospital social worker. Where, they wanted to know, was Carol supposed to go if she couldn't stay in the hospital and couldn't go home? As the social worker hunted for a place, the rules began to bend, slightly. A reason was found to keep her at NYU, a crack she could fall through . . . temporarily. Her pneumonia, something about adjusting her pain medication, whatever it was, it bought her another day, long enough for arrangements to be made for her to go to the Haven, an extended-nursing-care center and hospice, operated by the Visiting Nurse Service of New York, inside Bellevue Hospital, a few blocks away.

When I got to Carol's room on Tuesday around six P.M., Lissa was with her. "They're about to transfer her to the Haven. Should be any minute now." "Okay," I said, "I'll stay till they come. Who's *they*?" "An ambulance," Lissa replied. "When it arrives, someone will come and put her on a gurney and take her down. I'll ride along with her."

They seemed ready to go. Lissa gathered up Carol's things and put them in a plastic bag, which she parked on the bed. Carol was dressed in the clothes she was wearing when she'd arrived. Her discarded hospital gown was lying on a chair, strings hanging down. She looked pale and strained, obviously still in pain, but she managed her wolf grin. "The drugs work."

We caught up. We chatted. We looked at our watches. We asked a nurse who came in, "When are they coming?" Her answer: "They should have been here by now," but by seven o'clock, no one had appeared. At eight o'clock, we were still waiting. Carol was getting anxious. The message from the nurses' station was always the same: "They should have been here by now. We don't know what the problem is." At one point, I went to the ladies' room. I saw two men guiding a gurney through the narrow hallway. I rushed into Carol's room and told her. We heard it coming, getting closer, but then it didn't stop at her door. Maybe there was a mistake and it would be back, but no. It simply went away. None of us could think of anything to say. We stared at each other. Carol's sighs sounded like small gasps of pain.

She had a roommate, a young man, college age, from another country, although we never found out which one. He didn't seem to be sick. We wondered why he was there. His girlfriend was with him. They played video games on an iPad, cheering, laughing, calling out, making so much noise the nurses told them several times to be quiet. With each outburst, Carol winced.

Just before nine, I realized I couldn't wait any longer. My au pair was busy that evening, so I had to let Minnie and Harry out. Usually Minnie didn't eat her dinner until I got home. She would be hungry. Even if the buses came quickly, I'd be an hour getting home. Lissa said she'd stay. Carol protested, but clearly she was relieved she wouldn't have to make the move alone.

The next day, I called Lissa to find out what happened.

"We didn't get to the Haven till ten-thirty," she said. "It was pretty awful. The ambulance ride over there was rough. The driver went really fast, and the ambulance sort of tilted around corners. Carol bounced around a lot. She was in agony."

Carol agreed to go to the Haven because she was promised a single room. "Sure enough," Lissa went on, "when we arrived, she was put in a room with a roommate, an elderly woman who moans all the time."

The end of the excitement for one night? Hardly. No sooner had Carol been wheeled into her room than a palliative-care physician accompanied by an entourage of white-coated underlings of unknown function crowded around her bed with questions to ask and forms to fill out. All Carol wanted to do was go to sleep, but no. The questions came first. Finally they all left. Lissa started putting Carol's things away and making plans to go home. Suddenly, an aide materialized at the door and informed Carol she was about to be given a bath.

"We couldn't believe it. A bath? It was going on midnight," Lissa said. "This woman wouldn't take no for an answer. Carol kept telling her she'd already had a bath at NYU.

She didn't need two in one day. She just wanted to sleep. She was practically in tears. In the end, the woman left, but it was surreal."

The next morning, the palliative-care doctor was back with more mystery followers trailing after her, asking more questions, filling out more forms. She had no interest in the medications the NYU doctors had prescribed. She increased Carol's morphine dramatically, according to Lissa, turning her into a zombie.

I said I would be over after work.

If you want to find a hospital in Manhattan, go to the East Side. Hospitals line First Avenue, one after another for eighty blocks, their backs to the East River. Hulking monuments to specialization and philanthropy, with the names of their rich benefactors appearing in boldface on facades and over doors. Bellevue is toward the southern end of this crowded corridor. It's the oldest public hospital in the United States, dating from 1736, before the American Revolution, and it's huge.

I walked into the big glass entrance and asked how to get to the Haven. I was told, "On Seven. Down the hall. Follow the blue line on the floor." As opposed to lines in other colors, which led to different departments. All I could think of was Hansel and Gretel sprinkling bread crumbs along their path, leaving a trail so they might find their way home. The blue line went on and on, straight, to the right, then the left, past a restaurant, alongside a collection of amazing old photographs documenting Bellevue's history, for what must have been a quarter of a mile, until it stopped at a security desk next to an elevator bank, where I was given a visitor sticker. Over the next few weeks I would come to despise that blue line.

When I reached Carol's room, Lissa was there. Carol was so groggy from too much medication, she couldn't talk.

"And you know what else happened?" Lissa said after filling me in about the day. "In the middle of everything with her morphine, the 9/11 people came up to interview her. She knew it was important, but she was totally out of it."

The agency that monitors and evaluates 9/11 survivors had offices at Bellevue. To process Carol's claims for compensation, caseworkers needed to talk to her. For weeks they'd been trying to make an appointment, but her endless doctors' appointments had made scheduling impossible. Now here she was, so up they came.

Lissa described the visit. A whole new set of paper pushers with a whole new set of questions and forms. Carol practically unconscious in bed. "They asked whether she had her windows open on 9/11."

Carol emailed the following afternoon: "M— no visitors today, way too exhausted . . ." Then emojis: a sad face, a smiling face, a cat, lips, and a heart.

I sent new dog pictures. She replied with more emojis.

Then from Lissa, one of those which do you want to hear first, the good news or the bad news stories? How about the good news, because the bad news is *so* bad? The palliative-care doctor was finally working out the proper dosage for Carol's morphine and other medications, Lissa told me. So far so good, I thought. Carol's friend Kate, who was particularly good at confronting authorities, had managed to get Carol moved into the promised single room. Also good. *"But . . ."* Lissa got to the bad news, the unexpected bombshell. "Carol's being told she can't stay at the Haven. The doctor says if she can swallow pills on her own, hospice doesn't kick in, and Medicare won't pay."

It was NYU all over again. Suddenly I understood why she'd been taken off the drip she'd been on at NYU and been forced to take her medications orally at the Haven. It was a test.

"So now what?" I asked. Lissa sounded frantic. She and Kate and Cecilia, the Three Graces, were trying to figure out how to raise money, either to keep Carol at the Haven or to pay for twenty-four-hour home care. "We're trying to sell Carol's belongings. We're emailing all her friends about an online fund-raising campaign, too. You should have the email by now. If she has to go home, we've got to get rid of things, so there's room for a hospital bed."

Already, someone had agreed to buy her beautiful marble table. I tried to imagine her apartment without it and without all her other treasures. How would she feel if she went home and found the place pillaged, stripped of the things she loved? I reminded myself, How many thousands, how many millions, of Americans are worse off? I realized, I was missing the point, which was that three younger women who loved her were going to make sure, so help them, that Carol would get the care she needed.

"She's really upset." Lissa seemed pretty upset, too. "And I found out why her oncologist doesn't call back. She's technically on hospice now, so he's not allowed to have anything to do with her treatment anymore. Isn't that weird? I couldn't believe he was just ignoring her. I went along when she had her appointments with him. He's wonderful. I sort of had a crush on him."

I emailed Carol. "It just seems as if there's waaaayyy too much bureaucracy in all of this. I hate to put it this way, but your time is too valuable for all those doctors with conflicting, confusing information to steal it from you." Her response: "AMEN!!!!"

The next time I visited, Carol was propped up in bed holding a small, kidney-shaped, stainless steel basin in both hands in front of her, as if it were an offering. She was expecting to vomit. Odds and ends of sandwiches and pastries friends had brought her sat mostly uneaten on her bedside table, getting stale in crumpled-up cellophane, alongside plastic cups with bent straws and a water pitcher.

"I can't really eat. I've been getting sick to my stomach a lot," she said. "It's awful. Eating was always one of my favorite things." She didn't want to talk about what would happen if she was kicked out of the Haven. She wanted me to tell her about Harry and Minnie. Kate was there, too, regaling her with the gossip from their building, describing the doings of people I didn't know, exaggerating just enough, I thought, to make Carol laugh. The gossip she ate up as if it were dessert. Conversation stopped when a nurse came in with little paper cups on a tray, the kind you'd fill up with ketchup or mustard at a fast food restaurant. Each one contained a pill. Kate and I watched as Carol downed them with water. The nurse left. We started talking again. A few minutes passed, and then, a small miracle happened. A big miracle. Carol began heaving and then vomiting into the kidney-shaped basin. All of the pills she had just taken were floating in the runny mess she had thrown up. We stared at them for maybe five seconds. Suddenly, Kate snatched the basin out of Carol's hands and rushed out of the room. She took it straight to the nurses' station. I followed.

"Look at this! See?" Kate refused to be ignored. "Carol Fertig, down the hall, can't keep her medication down. I want to talk to her palliative-care doctor. Now! Here's proof she can't take pills by mouth anymore."

Carol was allowed to stay at the Haven.

FOURTEEN:
DOMESTIC BLISS

Carol was right. Harry, left to his own devices, would indeed have slept till noon every day. Unfortunately for him, chez Teichner, lying in bed all morning wasn't an option. At five-thirty, a quarter to six at the latest, when I usually get up, I'd find Harry against a pillow, perpendicular to my head, snoring. I'd slip out from under the covers, brush my teeth, wash, dress. Then I would collect the bag containing scissors, first-aid supplies, and the bootie I put over his cracked pad. Most days, he never woke up. He'd just keep right on snoring as I picked up his paw. It was like holding a baby's hand and waving goodbye. I could move it any way I wanted as I started applying antibiotic ointment and wrapping it in tape, eventually pulling on the red bootie and securing its Velcro strap. At night, after boosting Harry up onto my bed, I'd remove the bootie and cut the bandage off.

It took a while, but after considerable trial and error, I worked out a system and figured out which products worked best and how much of everything I needed to keep on hand.

I thought about what the people at my local CVS pharmacy must have thought. I would go in and buy them out of nonstick pads and the various kinds of tape I used, eight, ten, twelve rolls at a time, if they had that much, plus enough antibiotic ointment to oil an elephant. The girls at the registers always looked puzzled as I unloaded my basket. They had to recognize me, I was in there so often. Were they curious? Why those particular first-aid items over and over? What kind of injury were they for that never got better? How big was the person or thing this woman was patching up? Did she have a mummy at home?

They'd get in new stock, and suddenly, a day later, it would all be gone. Surely no other CVS store in Manhattan went through that stuff so fast. I could imagine the store manager looking at the sales figures and wondering what in the world was going on, the warehouse perplexed and possibly suspicious at the constant reordering. Every time, I'd shell out forty or fifty dollars. Harry's foot care, I discovered, was expensive.

Getting Harry up took some doing. A kiss or a pet might or might not wake him. Once he opened his eyes, his expression changed from trusting to suspicious to defiant. He never, ever, had any intention of starting his day when I started mine. He clearly preferred Carol's hours. Most mornings, he'd take one look at me and wriggle to whatever part of the bed was hardest for me to reach. I usually had to put my arms around him and haul/drag/push all sixty-something pounds of him along the duvet to the foot of the bed, then help him down to the floor.

Getting Minnie up in the morning was even harder than getting Harry up. She informed me daily that she was *not* a morning person. I'm quite sure she thought she *was* a person. I'd pull back her blankets and nudge her. No response. I'd nudge her again. No response. I'd pet her, scratch her ears. After three or four tries, *maybe* she'd raise her head and give me one of her indignant, put-out looks before pretending to go back to sleep. I'd try to lift her to a standing position. As often as not, she'd collapse back down again. When she finally deigned to leave her bed, on her terms, she'd arrange herself frog-dog style on a nearby rug and do several elaborate stretching exercises.

Breakfast. Not mine, Harry's and Minnie's. I ordered Harry's three kinds of prescription diet dog food online and had the shipments sent to my office, since delivery services can't get into the building where I live unless someone's home to buzz them in. A case of twelve cans and two eight-and-a-half-pound bags of dry food. Heavy. I took them home six cans or a bag at a time on the bus, so it took four days per shipment. I became a dog-food packhorse. In the morning, I mixed together some of each, plus big spoonfuls of Greek yogurt and canned pumpkin. I hid Harry's six different types of pills in wads of raw ground sirloin. Harry happily gobbled up his meals.

Minnie refused to eat unless she was hand-fed. She often refused to eat at all when I was away on assignment. She got bored with the same menu every day, so every couple of weeks, I pushed my grocery cart to the Barking Zoo and hauled home a fifteen-pound bag of something called Hund-n-flocken and an assortment of cans with such names as Grammy's Pot Pie and Santa Fe Skillet, in addition to plain old beef or venison or lamb. There was barely room in my pantry for what *I* planned to eat. Minnie, too, had yogurt and pumpkin with her breakfast, the pumpkin something new when Harry arrived. She seemed to like it, to the extent that she admitted to liking anything other than mangoes. Like Harry, she got her various medicines wrapped in meat. I found myself going through about six pounds of ground sirloin a week.

Hearing the litany of services rendered daily, a friend told me I must have a sign on my back, invisible to humans, that says FOOL FOR DOGS.

A walk. It was late fall and cold by the time Harry settled in, so after their breakfasts, I had to get both dogs into their sweaters or jackets. Harry cooperated. Minnie saw me coming and always ran around and around the apartment until I cornered her. If dogs can scowl, she was scowling.

Coffee in one hand, leash in the other, I urged the two of them down the front stairs to the street.

It was still dark when we went out. Sometimes, on clear mornings, as we made our way to Chelsea Piers and the park along the Hudson, I could see the moon just above the rooftops about to set, or a colossal cruise ship as tall as a building looming in front of us as we reached the water. I loved watching the ships glide by in the gloom on their way upriver to dock. Every day, I'd stop and sit on a particular bench so that I could say good morning to the Statue of Liberty in the distance, a bit hard to make out, but her raised arm and the white light of her torch unmistakable. Harry caught on quickly that this was our treat stop. Three treats, no more, except when I fell for the starving-dog act. Harry and Minnie had refined looking pitiful and hungry to an art, Minnie ever the actress. Harry was happy to be her leading man, especially if it meant a few extra treats.

I got into the habit of having my phone with me wherever I happened to be with the dogs. After Carol told me it would break her heart if I brought Harry to see her, I couldn't miss chances to take pictures to send her. Examples: standing at my feet in the kitchen looking up with expectation in their eyes; sitting together at the top of the stairs to the garden; lying on the floor, their bodies touching, her paws on his; Harry in bed; Minnie in bed; Harry and Minnie together in bed; Harry in his biker jacket; Harry in his varsity jacket covered with pins; the two of them tied to the wrought-iron fence across the street surrounded by a sea of fallen yellow ginkgo leaves; side by side squatting to pee directly in front of a sign with a picture of a dog in a circle with a line through it; three little birds perched inches away on the bench where I sat to hand out treats; Harry, his chin on the bench, eyeing the bag of treats just beyond his nose. That sort of thing.

Knowing I had to find pictures to take made me look around on our morning walks. I watched seagulls and cormorants bobbing on the river, riding a fast tide toward the ocean. Looking east, I saw a pink sky above a cubist cityscape, the Empire State Building a familiar face in the crowd, not the tallest but still tall in the geometry of dark buildings. As the sun came up, for a few minutes it turned the far side of the river, the New Jersey side, bright gold, the construction cranes and half-built high-rises transforming the New York side silver. Dawn felt spiritual. I needed those mornings.

For a few weeks, I saw a young red-tailed hawk every day. It would soar above the trees, then plunge suddenly, disappearing into the bushes before rising again, moments later, sometimes with a rat writhing in its beak. Often, it landed on a streetlamp overlooking the path the dogs and I took through the park. I never managed to get a good picture, but even in my sorry little snapshot, you recognize that this was a creature uninterested in the likes of us, its haughty profile silhouetted against the sky, its beak and head turned away.

On the walk home I strained to look in the windows of the art galleries. I checked out the posters advertising rock concerts and weird, trendy clothes plastered all over the plywood used to board up what was a restaurant before Superstorm Sandy destroyed it in 2012. New posters were slapped over old posters, their edges framed by an ooze of hardened glue. I couldn't pass the building without remembering what it looked like when the flooding drained away, the high-water mark left behind a foot above my head. Now homeless people slept in the shelter of the scaffolding that supported it.

The dogs had their own landmarks. Strange stones maybe three feet high, each one paired with a tree, line the 500 block of West Twenty-second Street, as if short druids had left behind proof they inhabited Manhattan once. In fact, part of a 1980s art installation, the stones have been repurposed. Peed on by practically every dog passing by, they are now the daily record of canine activity in the area. Harry and Minnie sniffed them, one after another, long and hard, reading them like a newspaper.

The more I looked, the more I was amazed by the extraordinary things there were to see on an ordinary walk.

Snacks. We came home and ate fruit together, something I've done with all my bull terriers. After I'd exercised, showered, and dressed, it was time for bite-size shredded wheat squares dipped in honey-roasted peanut butter.

Red kisses. Before I left for work or a trip, I'd give Harry and Minnie big, red lipstick kisses and tell them I loved them, some superstitious part of me hoping I was inoculating them from harm.

Dinner. Most nights, when I wasn't traveling, I'd get home from work around eight o'clock, say hello to the dogs, check the mail, change clothes, and then make dinner. If I lingered a little too long before heading into the kitchen, standing at my dining table opening bills or leafing through a magazine that had just arrived, Minnie — with her sidekick, Harry, in silent support — would bark at me, a loud, indignant, get-in-there-*now* bark. No ambiguity about her message whatsoever.

It's not as if the dogs were wasting away. My au pair made them dinner long before I got home. They wanted more dinner, some of my dinner. I would deposit bits of leftover meat or fish into their upturned mouths. With Minnie and Harry, I couldn't decide whether it was more like feeding baby birds or snapping turtles.

The farmers market. I was giddy on the Saturday Minnie and Harry and I set off for the farmers market together the first time, Harry wearing his red bootie. It was at the end of October, a few days after Stephen's emergency call asking me to take Harry for a few days; in fact, just a few hours before I found out he would be staying with me for good. There were again three of us heading to Union Square. Harry was lazy and had to be urged along. Minnie pulled a little. I had to be careful so that my grocery cart didn't run over their feet. It was a glorious morning, the market filled with apples and grapes, beautiful squashes and flowers, everywhere the colors of fall.

Arriving with Harry reminded me of going to school or work after getting a radically different haircut and feeling self-conscious, wondering what people would say or if anybody would even notice? I'd told a few regulars about Carol and Harry. Right about where I'd run into Stephen on that day in July, I now ran into Sunny and his owners, Mike and Julia. Minnie, as usual, ignored Sunny. Sunny lifted his head and wagged his tail slowly when he saw

Harry. They eyed each other and stood nose to nose. Carol once told me that Harry knew another bull terrier when he saw one. So, it seemed, did Sunny. Mike and Julia beamed.

At Cato Corner Cheese, the tall, lanky man who always cuts my slab of Dutch Farmstead into a tic-tac-toe of cubes to give to the dogs tipped a pile of free scraps into my palm and announced he was happy to make Harry's acquaintance. People did notice, and I wondered why it mattered so much to me that they knew the story and cared enough to be sad for Carol and glad for me.

FIFTEEN:
THE BUS AND THE RAIN

My memory of the last weeks of Carol's life is of near-constant rain. By mid-November, it was dark by four-thirty. At six or so, as I stood at the bus stop waiting, the wind and the wet and the cold, the night, made me angry. I hated trips to Bellevue. They were like going to hell on public transportation. I took the M57 crosstown to Second Avenue, then ran for the M15 heading downtown. Expressionless commuters dressed for winter sat in a fluorescent glare against fogged windows, their umbrellas dripping. I would try to stand just behind the bus driver, so that I could see where we were through the windshield. The wipers cleared arcs in the slick. It could easily take an hour or more to get from my office to the hospital, to the blue line on the floor. Why did I resent that line? It was just there to help people find their way. But following it on and on made me feel lonely and sad. I dreaded what I would find when I reached the seventh floor, when I got to the Haven, even though, for a while, visiting Carol seemed more like a gathering of friends enjoying one another's company than a death watch.

Usually, Lissa was there. One night, when I walked into Carol's room, Stephen was pulling photographs out of a folder. He had made eight-by-ten prints of a dozen or so of the pictures I had taken of Harry and Minnie. Carol was sitting up in bed, laughing, oohing and aahing over them. She had emailed me, "I live for these photos. Thank you." She said it again that night. The next time I visited, the prints of Harry and Minnie lined the wall across from her bed, taped so they were at eye level when she was lying down. The framed photograph of the mah-jongg group wearing their togas and gold laurel wreaths was propped against a box of tissues on her tray table. The lamp on Carol's nightstand was wearing her wreath. It circled the shade like a crown.

The following Sunday afternoon, when I got out of the elevator on the seventh floor, I was followed down the hall by several severe-looking people wearing drab clothing with equally drab looks on their faces. They stopped at the room next to Carol's, gathered around the bed, and began to sing softly. I couldn't make out the words or recognize the song, but I heard harmony and a hint of a descant above it, a pure sound, soothing, as sweet as the singers seemed sour.

Carol's door was closed. A handwritten sign was stuck to it: NO CLERGY, NO MUSIC, NO THANKS. FERTIG, C. Hmmm, I thought to myself. I knocked. I heard movement behind the door and then Lissa's voice: "Who is it?" "Martha," I called out. She let me in and shut the door after me. "What's going on?" I was perplexed.

"I don't want any of those people knocking," Carol said. I wondered which people. "Did I tell you about the Catholic priest?" she asked me. "No." "Well," she said as she raised the back of her bed. I could see that look in her eye, the old, pre-hospice Carol warming up to tell me a good story. "The other day, I was feeling really crappy. I was exhausted. At some point, a priest came in. I didn't even notice him. I must have been asleep. All of a sudden, there he was. He asked if I happened to be Catholic. I said no, I'm nothing. I practice no religion whatsoever, but I told him I was of Jewish origin."

Lissa had obviously heard the story. She

started shaking her head, incredulous still at what I was about to hear. "Guess what happened next?" I said I had no idea, knowing Carol fully intended to tell me. "He said to me, 'I'd like to give you a big blessing.' I said *no*. An emphatic *no*. I closed my eyes expecting him to leave. And *then*, I felt his hand touching my face and water running down my cheeks and neck. I heard him say, 'I baptize you in the name of the Father, Son, and Holy Ghost.' What on earth? I was shocked. I said, 'Get out, *now*.' I was furious."

Okay, that explained the NO CLERGY on the sign.

"*Then*, the same day, somebody comes in here and asks whether I'd like some music. I wondered what kind of music? You won't believe it. . . ." Carol looked straight at me through her big black glasses, a wicked glint in her eyes. She paused so I would be ready for the answer. "A harp!"

I laughed out loud, though *snorted* might be a better word. Lissa joined in. Carol made a face and started laughing, too. "Harp music for the dying. Is that preposterous? They want to get me ready for the pearly gates!"

SO NO MUSIC, NO THANKS, I figured, was an attempt at politeness, or not.

234

Over the next hour or so, Stephen stopped by and left. Lissa took a break and went to the family room down the hall to call home. I sensed some tension with her family over how much time she was spending at the hospice.

I was alone with Carol. Suddenly she reached for her kidney-shaped basin, held it up to her mouth, and began to retch. I said nothing as her retching turned into gagging. A minute went by, then two, maybe more. "This is a mess, such a mess," she whispered finally.

I said, "You're very brave."

"How so?"

"Because you've been clear-eyed about everything and because you've kept your sense of humor."

SIXTEEN:
THANKSGIVING

I stopped at three corner bodegas and rooted through all their flowers before buying an armload of hydrangeas to take to Carol. I stood clutching them at the bus stop, glad for a reason to hug my arms to my chest. It was damp and cold and gray, bone-chilling, bleak. The city seemed empty. Normally, I love the quiet of Thanksgiving in New York. Where was everybody? Hunkered down, cooking, gone out of town, watching the Macy's Parade on television or maybe the dog show? I watched the dog show for years, pumping away on my exercise bicycle, waiting and waiting to see the bull terriers being judged, but they were never shown. Maybe, if I looked hard, I'd see one or two BTs in the distance trotting around the ring with all the other terrier breeds. Enough was enough, so I gave up and stopped watching in protest.

The bus took forever to come. Hardly

anybody got on or off. There was no traffic, so it raced across town, with so few passengers, shaking and rattling as it sped along. It deposited me and my hydrangeas at First Avenue in less than ten minutes. Walking toward Bellevue, I dreaded having to pass the driveway where the Medical Examiner's Office's refrigerated body trucks were always lined up, like a mobile morgue. That day, though, I saw something beautiful there. A drift of fallen leaves had collected against the front tires of the closest truck, enormous sycamores. I picked one up. It was at least a foot wide, gold with brown speckles. I wondered whether I should take it to Carol, this perfect thing, this sunny embodiment of the autumn she was missing, her last. I admired it, but after a minute or two put it back down on the pavement and moved on. To this day, I wish I hadn't.

The plan was that I would visit Carol in the morning, and Stephen would come by in the afternoon. When I reached her room, someone else was there. The lights were off, and the shades were pulled down, so I couldn't quite see what was going on. Carol was propped up. She was groaning. Someone, a woman, was bent over her. With both hands, she appeared to be working a skinny rolling pin over Carol's neck and shoulders. "I've got a crick in my neck," Carol announced. The rolling pin turned out to be a battery-operated massage device, the woman wielding it, Ann Rittenberg, another of Carol's friends from her building.

Carol was alert and in a good mood, but I was startled at how she'd changed since I'd last seen her just four days before. She seemed much, much weaker, slightly desiccated, shrunken. Her skin looked tight on her face, the muscles in her neck sinewy. They stood out when she turned her head. Her eyes, behind the big black glasses, were glittery.

The three of us talked about Thanksgiving. Carol said, "Thanksgiving was always my favorite holiday." She used the word *was*.

I told the story of the first time I cooked Thanksgiving dinner for friends. It was 1974. I was working at a television station in Miami. My dining table sat *four* comfortably. I had *four* chairs. I had the little starter set of pale blue porcelain dishes for *four* my mother had given me, and cutlery for *four,* but I had invited nine people for a total of *ten* including myself. What was I thinking? I couldn't afford to spend a lot of money dealing with my predicament.

It happened that I was assigned to cover a school board meeting. On the way there with the cameraman, I noticed a shop window filled, and I mean *filled,* from bottom to top, side to side, with stacks of white china. A restaurant supply company. I shouted, "Stop!"

The prices were ridiculous, ten dollars a dozen for everything. You name it; I bought it: plates, bowls, serving pieces, knives, forks, spoons. Just as I was about to pay, I spotted demitasse cups and saucers and added those. They all said *TWA* on the bottom. For less than a hundred dollars, I solved one of my problems. I have most of the china still and use it, including the TWA cups. The airline stopped flying in 2001.

In another piece of luck, I noticed that the telephone company had been laying a lot of cable near where I lived, unrolling it from table-size wooden spools left by the side of the road. Late one night, friends with a pickup truck helped me liberate one of them. We put it on my balcony. If I covered it with some padding and a tablecloth, I thought, no one would get a splinter. I borrowed a few folding chairs and bought a few. One of the guests turned up on Thanksgiving carrying a large platter with a picture of a turkey on it she got at a thrift shop. I still use it, too. The dinner turned out well, and I was quite proud of myself.

Carol had a better story, a wonderful story. She said that for years she and several friends, including Stephen and his former boyfriend Paul, the Paul who crept into so many of Carol's and Stephen's conversations, would splurge and go to the Four Seasons restaurant for Thanksgiving, to wrap themselves in its glamour for an evening.

The restaurant is gone now, but for more than half a century, just the name conjured up a kind of movie New York, its population sleek and sexy, very grown-up in dinner jackets and gowns, the kind of people who sailed down Park Avenue in limousines, through a canyon of skyscrapers to the Seagram Building, Midtown Manhattan's modernist masterpiece, where the restaurant beckoned.

Everything about the Four Seasons restaurant was famous. Its architects, Ludwig Mies van der Rohe and Philip Johnson. Its iconic marble pool in the middle of one of its two rooms, ornamental trees in planters at each corner. As each of the four seasons began, the trees were replaced to reflect the time of year. Famously, a theater curtain painted by Picasso for the Ballets Russes divided the space. Famously and scandalously, the abstract expressionist painter Mark Rothko was commissioned to create a series of pictures for the restaurant but then refused to allow them to be hung there and gave back the money he was paid because its regular clientele included a who's who of famous names to be dropped, faces to recognize, the very people Rothko detested.

Carol smiled and described being offered champagne when she and her friends arrived for Thanksgiving dinner. They drank it by the pool and were then taken to another table for their meal. She talked about dressing up in clothes she had designed, choosing what to wear for the occasion and the place. A work of art herself, I could imagine her delight at being surrounded by objects made for the place, the tables, the chairs, the tableware, all of it custom, each detail considered. She said that every year she saw Helen Gurley Brown. Sometimes she'd be there already with her husband when Carol and her party arrived. Sometimes Brown would slip in just before they left. One way or another, until she died at ninety, the mother of the sexual revolution, the editor of *Cosmo,* the author of *Sex and the Single Girl,* would always make her appearance.

241

"But the best part, I think," Carol said, her lips quivering, the oxygen tube at her nose wheezing, "was every year getting a call from the restaurant, from Sophie. 'Miss Fertig, will you be making your customary reservation for Thanksgiving this year?' It was great." I thought, wow, the courtesy of that phone call. To be made to feel important enough, special enough, to be consulted before the reservation book filled up. Carol's smile crossed her face and touched her eyes as she remembered.

Soon her eyelids began to flutter and close. She was falling asleep. She asked Ann and me to leave. As I stood to go, I stroked her arm. It was damp and clammy, almost sticky, as it had been the last time I'd been there. I said to her, "This Thanksgiving, in addition to the things I'm always thankful for, I just want you to know, I'm very thankful for Harry and very thankful for knowing you, for this entire experience." She started to cry and mumbled, "Me, too."

As Ann Rittenberg and I reached the elevator, she started sobbing. Seeing Carol so helpless and uncomfortable, she told me, was unbearable. She and Carol had met when Ann moved to 15 Broad Street after her divorce. They'd only known each other for about three years, but Ann wished it had been twenty. "As I do," I said. We walked together the length of the blue line and then out onto the street before she stopped crying. I learned that she was a book agent, and that she was the person who was buying Carol's beautiful marble table. When we reached Twenty-third Street, she hailed a cab. I walked to the bus stop. We both had Thanksgiving dinners to attend.

The next morning, I got up at five-thirty and began cooking a second Thanksgiving dinner, this one for Stephen and another friend, John. I told both of them to arrive at 6:30 P.M. When I finally sat down for the first time all day, at about six, John showed up early. A little after seven Stephen phoned. I could hear his distress. His dog, Teddy, old and beginning to fail, was sick. Stephen had been out with him three times but was on the way now, he said. He arrived without the mashed potatoes he'd made. Worried about Teddy, he had left the dish on his kitchen counter in his rush to leave. I had baked sweet potato casserole because I like it, so there was no shortage of food. We had sweet potato casserole, turkey, homemade cranberry sauce, a green salad, and pumpkin chiffon pie with whipped cream for dessert.

Carol knew that Stephen was coming to my place for a belated Thanksgiving. She made me promise to send lots of pictures. I sent one of the turkey just out of the oven, another of the dogs staring up at the turkey, a couple of Stephen engaged in precision carving, me in an apron smiling next to the sideboard (taken by John), and a close-up of my plate. Carol was apparently waiting, phone in hand. Almost immediately, she emailed her pronouncement that the turkey was "gorgeous." After dinner, I sent a picture of Harry stretched out on the couch, sleeping off his share of the white meat. She replied, "Is football next?" Later I emailed her one last picture of Harry, standing in front of my open refrigerator studying the leftovers. In the subject line I wrote, "Better than football."

On Saturday, I woke up to the news that
Fidel Castro had died overnight, which
meant I would have to go to work and make
one final update to the obituary I had
updated over and over, every time the
former Cuban leader was seen in public or
was said to be ill. The trick with the obituar-
ies of famous people is that they have to be
done well before the individual actually dies.
No newspaper or television network would
dare wait until the death is announced
because it would be practically impossible
to assemble all the necessary interviews and
pictures fast enough to do a decent job. I
was assigned my Castro obit a good five or
six years before the fact, prompted by one
of the many rumors that Fidel was dead or
dying. It took weeks to research, write, and
put together. The producer, the video editor, and I joked after every false alarm, after
being called in to make changes every time

there was a new "Castro's dead" panic, that it was our doing that the guy was still alive, that we'd given him multiple new leases on life. At the rate we were going, we told ourselves, he would live forever.

But he didn't. Our obituary was running on *CBS Sunday Morning* the following day. Our executive producer would want to screen it again and approve our tweaks, but my shift at Carol's bedside was from two to six P.M. There was a schedule by then, informal, but the idea was to make sure that some member of her self-appointed family was with her most of the time, except during the overnight hours. Lissa kept track. She had become the gatekeeper. I texted her that I would go early and stay as long as I could.

Carol was alone when I walked into her room. The lights were off. In the gloom, all I could see were her giant, black glasses on a motionless mound at the far end of the bed, but she was awake. On the blanket beside her was a square plastic basin three times the size of the kidney-shaped stainless steel one it had replaced. For vomiting.

I talked about the dogs. "The city has been doing roadwork on Twenty-second Street between Tenth and Eleventh," I said. "Drilling. They've been pumping some sort of mucky slime into a tree pit on our route to Chelsea Piers. It's like a shiny black slurry. Harry couldn't resist. Yesterday morning, he walked right into it, all four feet. He sank down almost to his stomach. He was covered in it. His bootie was a mess. I had to use a wire brush to scrub it clean. Fortunately, my hose hasn't been turned off for the winter yet. You told me he hates hoses. Well, like it or not, he got hosed down yesterday, and the water was cold." I heard myself and thought, Too many words.

Carol opened her mouth and seemed to laugh at half speed. "That's my boy."

She told me she was uncomfortable. "Your back?" I asked. "No, my whole being." I cleared off her tray table, raised her bed, and brought her fresh water and ginger ale. Slowly, she lifted the plastic basin to her chest and waited, but nothing happened. Just as slowly, she lowered it. I poured her some ice water and held it up for her, but she grasped the cup and inched the bendy straw toward her lips. It collided with the oxygen tubes in her nose. For a good thirty seconds, she tried to guide it into her mouth. After a couple of small sips, she moved the cup back to her tray table, her hand shaking, as if it took all the effort in the world.

I didn't know what to say. I had used up all my words. Finally I asked, "When you're not overcome by your pain and discomfort, do you think about happy times or adventures? Do you relive parts of your life?" It was a question to fill the silence. I didn't expect much of an answer, but after a long pause, she mumbled something. "What?" I asked. Her voice came out a faint, high murmur. I heard, "Not really . . . pedestrian things." "Like what?" I asked. "The woods," she whispered, and went quiet. "Any woods in particular?" Pause . . . "The Adirondacks," she said, and smiled, just as she had on Thanksgiving talking about the Four Seasons restaurant, but now, two days later, she was much weaker.

Her story came out in breathy bursts that were hard to understand. Her ex-husband's family had a small house in the Adirondacks. She fell in love with the area when she went there with him. "There's a book." She strained to point toward a chair. I looked and saw a spiral notebook, on its black cardboard cover the words *Adirondack Days,* spelled out in twigs that had been glued on. One of the Three Graces, Kate or Cecilia, Lissa probably, must have brought it. I opened it and found a welcome letter. "Dear Miss Fertig and Violet." It was dated

August 4, 1996. The letterhead said "LAKE PLACID LODGE. A Classic Adirondack Retreat." On the page opposite the letter was a picture of Violet, Carol's first bull terrier, an over-the-shoulder shot taken from behind, a blue ball in her mouth. The image had been cut out and stuck to the lower right-hand corner of the page, arranged with a collage of other photos so that she appeared to be staring at a panoramic view of a building. A covered balcony extended over the porch. The railings were made of tree branches arranged to spell out: LAKE PLACID LODGE. On the next page was a photo of the word PINE mounted on birch bark and framed by twigs, the name of Carol's cabin, I guessed, because pictures of a stone fireplace and rustic plank walls came next, then lots and lots of Violet posing for the camera in bed, nestled against piles of pillows. The headboard, too, was a tangle of branches. Some folded note cards fell out as I turned more pages, each one printed with the same engraving of a deer next to a lake, Lake Placid probably, and a poem or quotation inside. From Samuel Johnson, for instance: "I would rather see the portrait of a dog I know, than all the allegorical paintings they can show me in the world." The cards must have been placed at

Carol's bedside every night when the maids turned down the sheets. Several said "Sweet Dreams." The one with the Samuel Johnson quote was signed "Happy Trails, Violet" in the same handwriting as the welcome letter from the hotel manager.

And sure enough, there were photos of Violet on a trail in the woods, bounding ahead of the unseen photographer (Carol), in some, looking back, seeming to beckon her, "Hurry up! Follow me!" And one of Violet crouching next to a dock. "She was objecting to my going in the water." I realized Carol must have been in the water looking back at the shoreline when she took the picture.

"What was Violet like compared to Harry?" I asked. Long pause. "She was a bitch . . . out for herself." That startled me. "They're very alike in some ways but very different. Harry is nicer." But clearly, she loved Violet dearly. Paging through the scrapbook, I found a snapshot of Carol on a bench, cradling Violet like a baby. It was the only picture of the two of them together. It wasn't glued in, so I turned it over and saw that it was taken in 1993, three years before the trip to the Lake Placid Lodge. Selfies didn't exist then, and there were no pictures of just Carol, which told me that she and

Violet had gone there by themselves.

I understood and recalled the sweet, contemplative melancholy I felt on trips I took alone. Loneliness scared me at first, but the loneliness didn't last. I found myself wider awake, seeing and smelling and hearing in a heightened way. For a change, I could pay attention to words and thoughts, worries and dreams, as they came and went in my head. Time felt like poetry. I could eavesdrop. I could pretend. I could forget. I could remember. I allowed myself the luxury.

Once, when I lived in England, I brought my first bull terrier, Piggy, with me on a long weekend. We took the train southwest from London to Dartmouth, a picturesque village in Devon tucked just upriver from the English Channel. Carol took a picture of Violet sitting in the front seat of a car as they drove to the Lake Placid Lodge. I took a picture of Piggy sitting across from me on British Rail, FIRST CLASS embroidered on the linen cloth velcroed to the seat behind his head. We stayed in a nice small inn. Piggy padded up several flights of stairs and, once we got to our top-floor room, picked out a red armchair as his. Instead of a walk in the woods, he and I took a public footpath that led us across a farmer's field full of sheep. Piggy had never seen sheep before. Sheep were among the great discoveries of his life, right up there with horses. He raced after them, straining at the end of his retractable leash, dragging me running along behind, holding on as best I could. The sheep had his number. They stood in twos and threes, staring at him as he approached. Whenever he got in lunging distance from any of them, they'd calmly trot a few feet to one side or another safely out of reach. Do sheep laugh? I had my camera with me. As I pitched and staggered, I managed a couple of one-handed shots of my crazy dog lurching out of control, truly at the end of his tether. In one, all four of his feet are off the ground. Suddenly, I saw that the field was about to come to an end. The horizon appeared just in front of us. It dawned on me almost too late that we were about to go over a cliff. I hauled Piggy back with all my strength and managed to reel him in a couple of yards from the edge. I looked down. The sea crashed over rocks hundreds of feet below us. When I saw how far we could have fallen, surely to our deaths, I felt faint.

The picture of Piggy in first class is in a frame next to my bed. I have no idea where the photos of our near-death experience in the farmer's field are now, in an envelope somewhere, stashed in a drawer probably. Why hadn't I ever made a scrapbook? Admiring *Adirondack Days,* I thought about how Carol told stories, and how I did. So different, the artist and the writer.

Carol struggled to breathe, gasping occasionally. She tried to reposition the little oxygen hoses in her nose. Finally, she asked me to get the nurse to increase the flow and to give her more of her nausea medicine.

Lissa arrived and gleefully announced she had gossip from their mah-jongg group. Cecilia's teenage son had been caught with his "fast" girlfriend attempting to undress her in his bed. When Cecilia discovered them, the girl ran to the bathroom half-naked. A serious discussion then took place between the parents. The Three Graces may have been goddesses, but they apparently hadn't given birth to angels. I saw a glimmer of devilment cross Carol's face. I stroked her arm, said goodbye, and went to work.

EIGHTEEN:
CONVERSATIONS ACROSS A DEATHBED

Carol's visitors were supposed to spell one another, but often they didn't leave when the next person showed up. They gathered around her bed talking to each other. When Carol was able, she listened and tried to talk a little, but usually drifted in and out of sleep. The conversations continued with and without her. At times, her friends forgot to be sad. Once, I walked in and found Stephen holding a phone to Carol's ear. It was playing Barbra Streisand songs. "She loves Barbra Streisand," he told me. Something about Carol reminded me of Streisand.

I was visiting her practically every weeknight and, on weekends, in the afternoons. Fortunately, I wasn't traveling much for work. I was writing stories that had already been shot. The 2016 presidential election was dominating the news cycle. Donald Trump seemed to be on every TV screen, all the time, the noise of the coverage a jangling constant. Except in Carol's room. Through the summer and into the fall, she had talked nonstop about politics, especially with Stephen, who, like her, was a news junkie. And with me, because I work in news. Now her TV was off. Her room was quiet. Going there was like entering perpetual twilight.

It was not unusual to arrive and find people I'd never met. Paul, Stephen's ex-boyfriend, the one who'd made up with Carol after they'd fallen out over a business deal. Michael, then editor of *Elle Decor* magazine, and his husband, Robert, a media relations consultant. Carol's friends Chuck, a pediatric endocrinologist at Sloan Kettering Cancer Center, and his partner, Jeffrey, a landscape designer, who'd known her since the 1970s. There were many more I didn't meet. Lee, the fashion writer, and Tony, her photographer husband, who came all the way from Australia. Carol's friend Charlotte from Portland, Oregon. Denise, the real estate heiress. Others, one after another, plus the regulars. Carol knew amazing people, a lot of them. Her gift for friendship.

Lissa was almost always there in the evening when I arrived. She put in long days. She admitted to me what I suspected, that her husband and daughter were upset because she was spending so much time with Carol. I could see their complaints upset her, but the need to be at Carol's side weighed on her more. And it was a need, but whose was greater, Carol's or Lissa's family's? Lissa couldn't bring herself to say out loud, "It won't be much longer. Carol will be gone soon."

One night it took me an hour and a half to get from my office to Bellevue. Rain pissing down. Nothing new there. Traffic a nightmare. Buses packed and steamy. I could feel rage rising in me. Walking the blue line, I noticed that giant plastic Christmas decorations had been installed halfway along the corridor, red-and-white candy canes, green and blue balls, a fake tree. When I reached Carol's room, she was asleep. Her mouth was slightly open, her long face tilted up a bit, her expression peaceful. Her chest, bony now, moved up and down as she breathed, the oxygen tubes in her nose hissing with each breath. She looked like a Renaissance painting of a tortured saint, ecstatic, transfigured by suffering and pain.

Lissa greeted me and said, "Look at this," then tapped and swiped at her phone. She handed it to me and smiled as I peered at a photograph. It reminded me of a 1970s record album cover. I saw a young woman in a beautiful lace-trimmed white dress. The sleeves were designed so that she seemed to be wearing a stole that had slipped off her shoulders.

"It's Carol on the day of her first wedding." I don't remember what I said, something unremarkable, *Huh,* or maybe *Wow* — whatever it was, totally inadequate to express my astonishment looking at the picture. In her arms, a magnificent bunch of calla lilies. Her veil resembled a mantilla.

"Her hair. I don't believe it," I said to Lissa. It was long and straight under the veil, chestnut brown. What did she have to do to get it that way? Rollers the size of frozen-orange-juice cans? Her eye makeup was dramatic. Lissa said she looked like Cher. I replied, "A combination of Cher and Barbra Streisand, styled by Frida Kahlo." I looked down at the bed. The Carol Fertig I saw there had short, gray hair, curly, springy, messy after being pressed against a hospital pillow for weeks. Her eyebrows were almost invisible, her lashes short. Where was the girlish woman in the picture? There somewhere. Carol told Lissa the bridesmaids had all worn white bonnets. I pictured the Pilgrims or *The Handmaid's Tale.*

Carol was married to artist David Fertig for eight years, according to Lissa. Carol kept his name when they were divorced because she was already known professionally as Carol Fertig. Her second husband's name was Fife. That's all Lissa knew. She hadn't contacted either of them. Carol's brother had come to say goodbye and said it wasn't necessary, that Carol wasn't in touch with them. Lissa was skeptical. "Her brother didn't even know Carol had a heart stent put in a few years ago. I looked him up. He's a toy designer. His name is John Fishman." She showed me his website. I saw wonderful, fanciful designs that made me marvel that a brother and sister could both be so talented in similar ways. "They didn't get along," Lissa said. I remembered that Carol did get along with his son. "They both came to see her. They were here for about a half an hour."

Another night, Lissa and Stephen and I all visited Carol at the same time. As we left, a nurse stopped us in the hall. She gave each of us a blue booklet, called *Gone from My Sight: The Dying Experience*. The cover had on it a pen-and-ink drawing of an old galleon sailing away, almost to the horizon line, its topsails already above it. It was an approximate guide, a what-to-watch-for timeline. "Any one of the signs in this booklet may be present; all may be present; none may be present," we read on page 1. "For some, it will take months to separate from their physical body, for others, only minutes. Death comes in its own time, in its own way."

We looked at each other and again at the book. It described a gradual withdrawal from the world, a loss of interest, a loss of appetite, of thirst. On page 5, the heading read, "One to Two Weeks Prior to Death." And then, "Disorientation." "Sleeping is most of the time now. . . . They may see and converse with loved ones who have died before them. There may be picking at the bedclothes and agitated arm movements. . . . Focus is changing from this world to the next; they are losing their grounding to earth." And so on. Then a list of physical changes to expect — to blood pressure, pulse rate, body temperature, breathing. What we might see days, hours, and finally minutes before death, then death itself. "Fear and unfinished business are two big factors in determining how much resistance we put into meeting death," it said.

I knew that from then on, we would be looking for those signs. I was sorry I'd seen the book because I didn't want to think about checking them off, counting down. The nurse told us that at some point Carol would be administered a "pain pack." She was getting morphine, but this would be more potent. Once it was activated, she would pass a point of no return. The nurse echoed the sentence in the book: "She'll be sleeping most of the time."

A week or so later, when I walked into Carol's room, Lissa was there with two more members of the mah-jongg group, Soniya and Jessica. I hadn't met them before. Jessica stood over Carol talking about her recent trip to Peru, to Machu Picchu, and then on to Chile, and the famous restaurant where she ate in Santiago that was "unbelievably pretentious. You sit through a fifteen-course tasting menu. During one course we drank a broth that was running through rocks. For dessert, we had to lick some sort of jelly off a twig." As everybody laughed at Jessica's story, even Carol, sort of, I said I wondered whether a server ever asked at the beginning of the meal, "Any allergies?" and was told, "Oh, I'm allergic to rocks."

Carol tried to form a word. She whispered, "Wa . . . wa . . ." Water. Lissa said Carol could only swallow a tiny bit of water from a cup by then. I tried to give her some. She choked on it. I rushed outside the door to ask Lissa how to do it right. She had stepped into the hallway with Jessica and Soniya to chat but was back in seconds. She raised the bed and held a cup of water to Carol's lips with her right hand, cradling Carol's back with her left as she sipped. I saw Lissa's efficiency, her skill, how gentle she was, how absorbed in what she was doing. She had learned just how high the bed should be, just where to hold the cup, so that Carol could swallow. A couple of weeks before, Carol had been drinking four big pitchers of ice water a day.

By the end of Thanksgiving weekend, on Sunday, her tray table was littered with what looked like cheese cubes on toothpicks at a cocktail party, except they were little sponges attached to sticks. Lissa showed me how to soak them in water and then hold them in Carol's mouth for her to suck but not swallow. Carol had crashed after I'd seen her the day before on my way to work. Her pain pack had been activated.

Lissa pointed to a box on Carol's window ledge. "Those are for you." Inside was the HARRY sign from his crate, a set of six mischievous-bull-terrier dessert plates, identical to a set someone had given me as a birthday present once, and goofy bull-terrier salt and pepper shakers. "You should take the *Adirondack Days* book, too." I had told Lissa about what Carol said. "How can I? It's so personal." Lissa shrugged. "Who else will understand what it means?" I wrapped the book in a large plastic bag, carefully, to cushion it, so none of the twigs glued to the cover would break off. I would treasure Carol's treasure. "Thank you." I wanted to say something profound but couldn't think of anything.

Another week went by before I could visit again. Work issues. On the afternoon of Sunday, December 4, when I walked into Carol's room for my shift, a stranger was sitting next to her bed, a slim, extremely well-dressed woman in a formfitting dress, who introduced herself as Camille Mc-Donald. She was chic. Her hair, auburn red, was styled but not too coiffed. Her makeup was perfect, understated. She and Carol had met long ago, she said, lost touch, then become friends again while Carol was doing licensing work for the designer Michael Kors. Camille was, at the time, CEO of LVMH Perfumes and Cosmetics in North America, the parent company of Michael Kors fragrances. Now, she said, she was president of brand merchandising for the chain Bath & Body Works. I liked her immediately. While Carol lay sleeping, we talked about trying to manage our complicated lives, about flying too much. She said that she was going home to pack for a flight that night to Saint Petersburg, Russia. She had meetings there and then more in Paris and London, all in less than a week.

Camille McDonald, supremely successful as she was, seemed tired of the travel, of the stress, of having so little control over her time, which is why, she said, she admired Carol so much. Camille talked about how much Carol had achieved, how broad and deep her talent was, how terribly she would miss her. "Her fierce individuality, that gift of friendship, her sense of fun. The kinds of things she did . . . Once she came back from Paris and, just for the look of it, pretended to smoke Gauloises for a while, because they were French." She recalled Carol's "wonderful dinner parties, all the interesting people. Her table was always beautiful, a work of art, especially in her earlier apartments, like the one that was in *Elle Decor* and the other magazines, before she moved to the studio. They were bigger." How many of Carol's friends had said the same thing? I felt jealous because I hadn't known her when she was having those parties.

Carol stirred. Camille and I took turns

trying to give her water, soaking the little sponges and holding them in her mouth.

Camille looked at her watch and sighed. She gathered up her bag, put on her coat, and kissed Carol goodbye. It was a real goodbye, a last goodbye, not "Bye till I get back."

I was alone with Carol for maybe an hour. I held her hand. Her grip was still surprisingly strong. I noticed that her skin was soft and dry, not sticky or moist anymore. I gave her water when she woke up and talked to her about the dogs. I said that in a couple of weeks I was going to be taking them with me to South Carolina for Christmas. It would be Harry's first flight. I don't know how much she heard. Weeks before, on one of Harry's "dates" with Minnie, I had told her about the house I have near Charleston on a barrier island. I bought it for my mother and then kept it after she died. Harry would get to go to the beach with Minnie. I imagined them romping together in the sand, Harry chasing after Minnie as she frolicked happily in the ocean. I wondered how I'd deal with his red bootie, whether to let him get it wet or pull it off before we reached the end of the boardwalk.

Carol had said, "If he takes after me, he'll hate the beach." I smiled, remembering.

She was flinging her arms out away from her body, one of the signs described in the blue booklet under "One to Two Weeks Prior to Death." Her sheet was pulled down. Her hospital gown had come undone, so her breasts were exposed. It hadn't bothered Camille and me, but I decided to call a nurse to help straighten her bedclothes before Alan Wade showed up to take my place. One of Carol's friends I'd met at the party on the roof of 55 Hudson Street, Alan had the next shift. We sat for a while together.

He, too, went on and on about Carol's wonderful dinner parties, all the fun, her marvelous table decorations, her terrific eye. Then he said, "It's too bad she never really succeeded." After what Camille had just told me, I was stunned. "Christian Dior's partner had a business brain. He knew how to make Dior a brand. That's what Carol needed. She just needed someone to turn what she did into a real business." What Camille had seen as achievement, Alan saw as not quite making it. How could two people look at a career, a life, so differently? "She got taken advantage of and actually swindled, too." Apparently, she had allowed a lawyer, a kind of business-manager-to-the-stars type, to manage the money she made

265

when things were going well for her. He systematically stole from his clients, including Carol, leaving her in financial difficulty. He went to prison, Alan said, but Carol didn't get her money back. Suddenly I understood her moves to steadily smaller apartments. I said I thought she *was* successful. Alan replied, "But she should have been famous." I wondered if she could hear us. She appeared to be asleep, beyond knowing, beyond caring.

It was two days before I could visit again. On Tuesday, December 6, when I saw Carol, I realized she had slipped badly since Sunday. Her breathing was labored and erratic. Her face was contorted; her fists were clenched. She was clearly in pain, but I was sure she was awake and aware. Lissa left the room for a while, so I was alone with her.

I said, "It's all right to go. It's okay to stop fighting. Harry is fine. He loves you, but I'll love him, too, with all my heart, and will protect him and care for him as long as he lives, and then you'll have him back. Go and join Violet. She's waiting for you in the woods."

A nurse came in and gave her an injection. Her forehead relaxed.

I got as far as the elevator before I started to cry. I cried as I walked the endless corridor out to First Avenue. I looked for my umbrella but had left it somewhere. It was raining, raining on the tears rolling down my cheeks.

NINETEEN:
THE END

I couldn't understand it. The next day, I was restless, uneasy. It was hard to concentrate. Why? I know this sounds kind of woo-woo, but it was as if a voice inside me were whispering, "Go, go now to Bellevue," while the creature of habit in me said, "Oh, I'll go after work, as usual," and then that other voice started shouting, *"No, go now!"* Good thing it did.

Around four in the afternoon, Lissa sent out a text saying that Carol was in a lot of distress and "they," I suppose the nursing staff, were advising no visitors that night. By then, I had made up my mind to go anyway. It was a little after five when I replied that it was too late. I was on the bus halfway there already.

I looked at my watch as I walked into Carol's room: 6:05 P.M. It was obvious she was dying. Her breathing was shallow, the intervals between breaths getting longer and longer as the minutes went by. Her life was leaking away.

Four of us were at her side: Lissa, of course; Chuck Sklar, Carol's friend who is a pediatric endocrinologist at Sloan Kettering; Kate, another of the Three Graces; and me. We sat in the pool of light from the lamp that still wore Carol's gilded laurel wreath, surrounded by darkness. Each of us, in turn, told her we loved her. I added, "Don't worry about Harry. I promise I'll take good care of him." Lissa and Chuck stroked her hands, Kate and I the lumpy white bedspread covering her legs.

By six-thirty, it was over, but we didn't stop. When she had been dead long enough for all of us to understand that she was truly gone, that another breath would not come in a second or a minute, Chuck stood up to leave, kissed her on the forehead, and said to the rest of us, "To be with someone at the moment of death is a privilege." Yes. I'd never thought about it that way, but yes.

Lissa, Kate, and I sat in silence, until suddenly we were startled by a disturbance at the door. Stephen, with his dog, Teddy. Lissa had called him when it was clear that Carol was dying. His entrance felt like an explosion. He stopped a few feet from Carol's bed, saw us, saw Carol, and took in that she was dead. We retreated, so he could have his time with her. I took Teddy's leash.

Stephen held her hand and kissed her. He bowed his head. After about a minute, he sighed. "I can't," he said. "I can't do this." His chair scraped on the floor as he lurched to his feet and backed away.

Carol's stillness had cast a spell over us, just long enough, maybe, for her soul to wisp away, and now the spell was broken.

Stephen explained he had been caught in traffic. "It's raining," he said. Lissa and Kate switched into task mode, Three Graces mode, and began pacing the hallway phoning Carol's friends and her brother, delivering the message that she had died, one short, matter-of-fact conversation after another. They spoke quietly, calmly, their pain hidden. Lissa set in motion having Carol's body collected by the funeral home.

I watched this and remembered a story I did years ago, while I was based in South Africa. I was sent with a crew and a producer to a tiny village near Durban to cover a massacre. Thirteen people dead, seven of them children, the victims collateral damage in tribal fighting between Zulus and Xhosas. The man the killers were after wasn't even there. They had gone to the wrong house. When we arrived, the bodies had been taken away. A few gawkers stood around still, but mainly to see us. One of them said, "Hey, you're too late. Nothing left but women's work." He pointed to the whitewashed concrete building behind him. There was blood everywhere, running down the walls, smeared on the threshold, in pools on the ground outside the door. A half dozen or so older black women, heavyset, in loose dresses, their heads wrapped in scarves, grandmothers, were washing it away. They sang as they bent to wring out rags in buckets, over and over, the water running pink. Their harmonies were beautiful and sad.

My producer and crew said to one another, "Okay, okay, no story, let's get going." I turned to them. "*This* is the story." I nodded toward the women. With dignity and true grace, they did their "women's work," as women always have in the aftermath of death, trying to bring order to what they cannot make right. And so it was with Lissa and Kate.

The nurses said they would wash Carol's body and brush her hair before she was taken away, but she would have to lie in place for four hours before anything could happen. Regulations. Had some patients started breathing again, come back to life?

"Go home," we were told, but Lissa refused. She sat down next to Carol's bed and began sobbing, her composure at last spent. She kept repeating, her voice a strangled whisper, "Where will I go tomorrow? Where will I go tomorrow?"

Stephen said, "It's time. I'll drive everybody home." Lissa covered her face with her hands and shook her head.

Kate peeled off the pictures of Harry and Minnie taped to the walls, lifted the laurel wreath from the lamp, and was gathering up the rest of Carol's belongings when she spotted the wheelchair in the corner. "That's the one hospice delivered to her apartment, right? The one you brought her to NYU Hospital in?" She looked to Stephen and then to Lissa. They nodded. "I'm sure we can just leave it here," Stephen reasoned. "This is hospice, too."

Wrong. A nurse informed us, "Oh, no, you have to take it back to where it was delivered and have it picked up there." Why? "Because that's a different hospice. Hospice Home Care. They have to pick it up wherever they delivered it in the first place."

"And they can't pick it up here?" Stephen asked.

"No."

Blessed bureaucracy.

Kate stood behind Lissa, put her arms around her shoulders, and gently helped her to her feet.

Leaving was tedious, a clumsy, logistical mess: pushing the empty wheelchair to the elevator; retrieving Stephen's car from the parking lot; shifting the stepladder, the grocery cart, and the rest of the clutter in the back seat to make room for passengers; folding the wheelchair and wrestling it onto the dog bed in the back; boosting Teddy up next to it. In the rain. Stupid, ordinary stuff, absolutely infuriating in that moment.

Stephen missed the turn we were supposed to take out of the hospital parking lot. We had to circle all the way around Lower Manhattan to get to Carol's building. I think he must have been distracted and forgot about the security checkpoint in front of the NY Stock Exchange blocking our way. He jerked to a halt beyond the stop line, inches from where the steel jaws rose from the street, glinting in the light of a streetlamp. Armed guards leaped up. They searched the car. Their sniffer dogs sniffed Teddy. We were waved on. At 15 Broad Street, little was said. We took turns hugging one another, then Kate and Lissa turned away. The automatic doors parted. They walked into the bright lobby light pushing the wheelchair.

Stephen announced he was running out of gas. I thought he meant he had had it, that Carol's death, that all the driving, the missed turn, the fuss over the wheelchair, had gotten to him. It was getting to me. "No, I'm not sure I have enough gas to get you home, certainly not enough to get myself home. We have to find a gas station." Easier said than done. Gas stations in Manhattan have been disappearing, poof, like magic, turning into high-rises. The ones Stephen remembered from before he moved uptown were all gone, we discovered, as we drove around in the rain watching the needle on the gas gauge edging closer and closer to empty. Shall we say, a drama ensued. I imagined a comic book word bubble full of *X*'s, hashtags, lightning symbols, and exclamation points right above my head but did not swear out loud. This wasn't Stephen's fault. He found out that Carol was dying, jumped in his car, and thought of nothing other than getting to Bellevue.

The night turned strange. I don't have a car in the city but remembered the BP station I passed every morning riding the bus, on Tenth Avenue around Thirty-seventh Street. "Can we make it that far?" Stephen looked at me. "We'd better."

Heading west on Fourteenth Street, though, traffic was stopped at Eighth Avenue. There we were blocked by a huge late-1950s Cadillac, a magnificent sight, all chrome and fins, raindrops glistening all over it, but stalled. Unbelievable. How could this be happening? I thought. The driver shouted out the window, "Do you have jumper cables?" Stephen shouted back, "Yes." After a minute or so of rummaging in his junk drawer of a back seat, he held out the ends of the cables in both hands with a big smile, as if he had captured a snake. Of course, his motor was still running, drinking gas, as he attached the clips to the batteries of both cars. It was another five minutes before the Cadillac would run on its own. More gas gone. What next?

We turned right onto Tenth Avenue, at a corner where there used to be a lovely big gas station that even had a car wash. No more. It was boarded up.

I began to relax, only twenty-three blocks to go, a straight shot. We cruised along, past Twenty-second, my street. I could have just gotten out and walked home, but Stephen said that he wanted to see Harry. Then around Twenty-ninth, we hit traffic, bumper-to-bumper, nobody moving. Stephen pounded the steering wheel. Ahead of us, above the cars, the long neck of a construction crane, like some sort of mechanical giraffe, but bigger, was nodding its way across Thirty-fourth Street. Could this actually be happening? I wondered. It seemed so weird, unreal in my state of mind.

"Hudson Yards," I said. Stephen grunted. An 18-million-square-foot office and residential development, Hudson Yards was under construction just where we were stranded, practically in sight of the gas station. We sat, panicky now, idling. Stephen switched off his engine until finally, ten minutes later, a few cars began to move. Others jostled as they tried to merge and follow single file. Inching our way north, we could see giant girders being unloaded from flatbed trailers taking up two of Tenth Avenue's six lanes. The crane took up three more, as it began lifting a girder skyward. A man in a reflective vest and a hard hat raised a stop sign, then allowed us to creep past. Three more blocks, I kept thinking, three more blocks.

"Yes!" Stephen called out when we reached the gas station. Cars were backed up behind every pump. A taxi was in front of us. The driver, a man with a white beard, wearing a white ankle-length robe and white crocheted

skullcap, stood next to it waving his arms. When the pump was free, he made no effort to get back in his car and move ahead. We waited. The man continued to wave his arms. "What's he *doing*?" Stephen pounded the steering wheel again and yelled out the window. I watched as he got angrier and angrier. Suddenly, he flung open his door, jumped out, and strode over to the taxi driver. Through the windshield, I could see the scene unfold, Stephen confronting the man, his chest out, arms up. I thought he was going to haul off and hit him, but suddenly he stopped, stepped back, and wiped his forehead with his hand, realizing the taxi had broken down. The driver was trying to warn him off. I watched Stephen implode, the rage drain out of him. He apologized. The old man bobbed his head, said something, and pointed at his taxi. Together, they pushed it out of the way. We got our gas and drove off. Two stalled cars in one bizarre night, a night that felt like a hallucination. At least the rain had stopped.

We pulled in by the fire hydrant across the street from my building. I brought Harry outside. At the sight of Stephen, he turned into a wagging, jumping, kissing, four-footed frenzy. Stephen dropped to his knees, held Harry in his arms, and wept into his fur.

It was ten o'clock. Carol had been dead three and a half hours.

TWENTY:
AND THEN WHAT?

I think the real reason Stephen wanted me to go with him to Carol's apartment the following weekend was dread. He said I needed to go through the rest of Harry's belongings and decide what I wanted and what should be given away. How many more belongings could one dog possibly have, stashed in a studio apartment? I was convinced Stephen couldn't bear going into Carol's space alone. On the drive downtown, he said he hadn't been there since the day she had fallen, the day he and Lissa took her to the hospital. Stephen was one of two executors Carol chose to handle her estate, friends she picked because she considered them family, part of the family she'd assembled for herself. His job was to make sure objects she had promised to particular people got to them, then to sell the rest of her valuables through his interior design contacts or at auction. Some things he had to find and deliver, others he had to photograph. "I have to go right away because Carol's rent is only paid through the end of the December. Everything needs to be out by then."

We stopped in the lobby at the oversize, Louis-something-or-other-style reception desk, where doormen oversaw the comings and goings in the building. As we collected a key to Carol's apartment, we noticed the framed death notice on the marble top. In the center, a photograph of Carol sitting on a low stone bench in her enormous Russian fur hat, earflaps down, only her smile and her glasses visible, Harry's bowl and balls beside her. Harry, wearing his varsity jacket covered with pins, stood in front of her, staring at the camera. It was her favorite picture of herself with Harry, the one she used to say goodbye the last time she posted her art blog, *Object-Lesson.* To the right of the photo, the *Object-Lesson* logo, the antique engraving of an eye, colored bright blue. To the left, her armorial with its crown and little flags topped with whimsical creatures. The notice read, "Carol Fertig passed away peacefully on December 7, 2016, surrounded by loving friends. Harry Fertig was adopted into a new home outside the building, and is thriving. Thank you to all who reached out to her during her brief illness.

Your kind words and gestures were much appreciated."

Lissa, I thought. She did that.

When we walked into the apartment, Stephen inhaled loudly. His voice caught as he said, "I can smell Carol's perfume." I felt her absence, not her presence. I saw the gilded party chair I had admired the first time I'd visited, its seat upholstered in bull terrier fabric. I noticed that the beautiful marble dining table Carol's friend Ann Rittenberg had bought was still there. So was the cupboard Carol had collaged with fragments of ideas and inspirations, of no use anymore. What had been expressions of Carol's tastes, her passions and pleasures, were only artifacts now. The Carolness of the place was mostly missing. The bookshelves were empty. Her tremendous library of art and fashion books had been packed up and given to the Fashion Institute of Technology. Many of her clothes were gone. Stephen was looking for a piece of Venetian glass. As he searched, he would pick things up and tell me their stories, seeing the past, but I felt like a detective inspecting clues to a disappearance. I was a voyeur. Next to Carol's computer, I noticed a piece of paper taped to the wall, a list written in black marker. Crossed off, "Halloween candy" and "ship box," among other things. Farther down, still to do: "memorial," and below that, "Marthabook homework," then "codes & passwords," followed by "clean desk, organize winter clothes," and "9/11 Appt? 2nd or 20th."

In the middle of the room were neat piles of boxes and garbage bags, labeled. Lissa and Kate had been here already cleaning and organizing. Carol had died on Wednesday. It was Saturday. Harry's wire crate stood next to the "Martha" pile. "Do you want it?" Stephen asked. "No, give it away. I can't fly him to South Carolina in that kind. I can in his new one." Rummaging through the contents of my pile, I discovered that Harry had vastly more clothes, tennis balls, collars, leashes, harnesses, toys, and bones than I had already been given. Where on earth had Carol been keeping them all?

Then I came across a largish muslin drawstring sack, a note from Lissa sitting on top: "Carol wanted Martha to have this." Inside, I found a designer handbag that I knew from the name had to have cost a couple of thousand dollars. It had a brown leather handle strap and was roomy but definitely not utilitarian. It was covered with thousands of black loops, made out of narrow ribbons of plastic, like loopy linguine, I thought. It was odd but undeniably chic, very Carol, a bag that was fun. I would never have bought something so extravagant, so out there, for myself. I own maybe three handbags total, my good, dressy one thirty years old. Now this one was mine. I opened it. Spotless. No Kleenex shreds or rubber bands, stray pennies or sticky old cough drops, the kinds of things in the bottom of my other bags. Carol had clearly used it but had taken good care of it, cleaned it out, plumped it up to keep its shape by stuffing it with wadded tissue paper. Why this? Why me? Suddenly, I knew. I remembered a night Carol had brought Harry to see Minnie. Over dinner, we talked about fashion, what we liked, what we didn't. I recalled showing her the expensive black jacket I had bought and how she had examined the cut and the detail and had smiled her approval and how she had said, "I have just the bag for that jacket." At the time, I wondered what she was talking about. That night she also told me about a man who photographs dogs.

I felt in the zipper pocket of my new bag and found his card.

A week after Carol died, Harry and Minnie and I flew to South Carolina for the holidays. I packed Harry's bowl and balls, plus two sweaters and one of his jackets, in my suitcase, figuring it would turn cold. I folded his giraffe rug in half and put it in his crate so he'd have something soft and familiar to reassure him during his first flight. Minnie had a fat, squishy pillow covered in shag inside hers. My little frequent flier, she had flown at least thirty times in the nine years I'd had her. I packed sweaters and a jacket for her, too, along with a thick braided-rope toy, so the dogs could play tug-of-war. I ordered all three kinds of Harry's prescription dog food so they would be waiting at the door when we arrived. I told him what fun we all would have.

Minnie loved the beach. She would race to the top of the dunes and jump off. I'm convinced she thought she could fly. She adored splashing through the little waves that lapped the sand, bodysurfing up to her neck, plunging into the deep pools that collected as high tide approached. The bigger the pools, the better she liked them. Sometimes the water was over my head. I worried about her trying to swim across. She wasn't young anymore. As she paddled along, a tiny white thing in the distance, too far away for me to catch up to her, I'd pray she wouldn't drown as I ran around to the far side. When I pulled her onto the bank, into my arms, she would look at me as if she'd just successfully crossed the English Channel.

Every dog I'd brought to the beach loved it. At the end of Goose's life, because of his heart condition, he couldn't walk very far. I bought him a wagon with a removable side panel, so I could lift him into it. I'd pull him down the boardwalk. Once we got to the end, he could make his way slowly to the water. He'd lie down in it and let it wash over him while Minnie scampered around.

I loved the beach, too, summer or winter, good weather or bad, so I could hardly wait to take Harry.

When we reached the end of the board-walk, I took off his red bootie but left the tape and wrappings on, so his cracked pad wouldn't hurt when he walked. He stepped into the soft sand. It moved under his weight. He stopped, looked down, then up at me. I tugged his leash a little. He resisted. I tugged again. He began walking, stiff legged, like a pull toy. Shifting sands were clearly not his thing. I could imagine him asking himself, "What is this? Where's the sidewalk? I'm a city dog." He stopped to sniff some seaweed and a piece of driftwood. He considered a dead horseshoe crab. It looked like a miniature tank turret turned upside down. He peed in it. When I led him into the water, water maybe two inches deep, he jumped back, surprised. I could see he considered this a bad surprise, not a good surprise.

My father had an expression for people who are finicky about roughing it, fussy about encountering insects or wildlife in the woods, unhappy with anything other than five-star luxury. He called them "hothouse tomatoes." Harry was a hothouse tomato.

I remembered what Carol had said when I told her Harry would be going to the beach: "If he takes after me, he'll hate it."

Stephen and I spoke and wished each other a happy New Year. He laughed when I told him about Harry and the beach. He told me that everything was out of Carol's apartment. He'd been there every day, going through her things. He'd also gone through her storage unit. "I have more stuff for you. I'll bring it over when you're back." More? Impossible.

I asked how he was holding up. "I miss her. It's been hard seeing the apartment empty. I've gotten the things that are going to be sold cataloged and off to the auction house. Pretty much everything that's supposed to go to someone has gone. Whatever else that needs to be kept, I've taken home, lots of papers and files."

"Is the photograph still up in the lobby?"

"No. It's been taken down."

The Carol Club had disbanded. The people she'd brought together with her gift for friendship had carried their memories away with the keepsakes they had inherited.

I had Harry, the most precious of all her bequests.

TWENTY-ONE:
BAD NEWS

I think Harry was happy. I watched him, looking for signs that he was pining for Carol the way Minnie had pined when Goose disappeared from her life. I thought maybe he would stop eating or mope on his bed as weeks went by and nobody took him home to her. It didn't happen. I expected him to ignore me when I walked in my front door at night, but not long after he came to stay, he began wagging his tail and dancing around when I said hello to him, as if he was glad to see me. And he licked my toes. Before I'd even met Harry, Carol emailed "a warning" that he was a "toe licker." One night when they came over for dinner, I heard a rhythmical noise under the table, like loud, steady smacking. I bent down and saw that Carol had taken her shoes off, and Harry was hard at work. I couldn't imagine him transferring his loyalties, indulging his foot fetish on anyone other than Carol, but he did. All I can say about that big soft tongue slipping back and forth between my toes is . . . think about being tickled as a kid, so hard you wanted to scream.

Harry seemed to fit right in. I asked Dr. Farber, the vet, why he thought Harry was adjusting so well. His answer: "Minnie." I thought about the way she teased Harry. It looked like flirting to me. And how he watched her perform, how he followed her around, used her as a pillow when they napped together, deferred to her when they wanted to go in opposite directions on their walks. When Goose was alive, he was the alpha dog, no matter how much Minnie wanted to call the shots. Now the girl who thought she was a glamorous movie star or maybe a princess could be queen. Harry was her subject, but no doubt about it, also her prince. She was ecstatic. I'd never seen her happier. The arrangement suited him, too. He found everything about her fascinating, particularly her habit of "hitting the sack," my description for the way she worms her way into my stiffened-canvas laundry bin, which I leave tipped over on my bedroom floor for her. Harry would stand by looking puzzled while socks and underpants and T-shirts flew out and landed at his feet as she squirmed around. It didn't take him long to decide *he* wanted to try out her sack when she wasn't in it herself, when she was sleeping on my bed under the covers, for example. Unfortunately, he was too big. I'd find him standing with his head and front paws inside, stuck. Sometimes I'd take pity on him and pull him out. He was determined, though, and finally, one day, I couldn't resist shooting video of him at it. I was laughing so hard I could barely hold my phone still. He'd gotten almost all the way in but couldn't figure out what to do then. Turning around was impossible. It took him several minutes to extricate himself.

Laughter was easier with Harry around. After Goose died, I stopped laughing much, even though I had Minnie to love. Carol's illness and death didn't help. Watching Harry and Minnie together, I stopped thinking about loss. Every single day, I had two funny dogs to enjoy. The present was a wonderful place to be with them.

I'm reluctant to admit what I'm about to say next. To fill the time on walks, over the years, I've made up absolutely ridiculous, silly stories about my dogs. I thought of them as children's stories, but children might find them too weird. Once Harry had come for good, it was time to incorporate him in the one I'd invented around Minnie. So, here goes.

Listening to the radio, every so often I'd hear that some program or other had been sponsored by an email marketing company that featured "drag-'n'-drop" technology, which sounds like "dragon drop." Minnie, who, everyone knows, thinks she's a princess and is very beautiful, likes to attend Dragon Drops, which resemble Renaissance fairs, with jousting and so on, except that they also involve dragging dragons to the tops of cliffs and dropping them over the edge. In the New York area, she tells me, they take place along the Hudson River at the Palisades. Since dragons can fly, a Dragon Drop is a fine opportunity to take a wild ride. Minnie, so the story goes, is better than anyone else at wrangling dragons, urging them to the cliff edge and, then once they've landed later, rounding them up. She is also an accomplished dragon rider, who favors a jeweled sidesaddle. Now when Harry arrives on the scene, she's got to figure out what to do with him. Taking him to his first Dragon Drop, she discovers that because he's a city boy, he isn't at all comfortable around dragons, so she enrolls him in shape-shifting classes taught by wizards. Dragon Drops are more magical than Renaissance fairs. Somehow, at his next Dragon Drop, he finds himself in Advanced Shape-Shifting. Because he didn't pay attention during Shape-Shifting 101, he makes a grave mistake and turns himself into half a flamingo, the front half of him a pink, long-necked bird, the back half, a dog. Minnie is distraught when she gets back after wrangling all the dragons and discovers this disaster. It takes all her charm and skill to convince the wizards, who are doubled over in hysterics at Harry's transformation, their pointy hats pointed every which direction, to change him back to his normal self. Embarrassed, Harry says that in the future he'd prefer to stay home.

It felt as if I had the license to include Harry in the nonsense. It was fun. Everything was good. I was happy again . . . and then . . .

On what would have been Carol's seventy-first birthday, Thursday, January 19, 2017, Harry was diagnosed with cancer.

For several days, he'd been sick with some sort of dog flu, which began with nonstop vomiting. Then came nonstop diarrhea. Cleaning him up after a bad night, I discovered a swelling on his behind. It was ugly, raw and fiery red, bloody. It hadn't been there the last time I'd washed him off, maybe a day before, two at the most, and it scared me. Cancer, I suspected. No, I knew it was cancer. Minnie sniffed him as if she knew, too.

Harry, always terrified of going to the vet, tried to dive under my legs as I sat in the exam room, but the space below the built-in bench was too small. Only his head and shoulders fit. Just as he did when he tried to get in Minnie's sack, he misjudged how much of him would stick out. It would have been funny any other day. Lifting him onto the examining table took every bit of the vet tech's strength. Solemnly, Dr. Farber aspirated the lump with two different needles to get two separate tissue samples, but I could see he had no doubt. He had known Carol for more than twenty years, all of Violet's life and now Harry's. Her death had been hard for Dr. Farber to take, but the consolation was that he had been part of the silver-lining story of how Harry ended up with Minnie and me. We were all supposed to live happily ever after, right?

Why does bad news always arrive as a storm surge, rather than a few drops of rain? Backing up, it all started just before the New Year. The dogs and I were in South Carolina for the holidays, about to head back to New York City.

Speaking of dogs, the cliché "sick as a dog" kept running through my mind. I had a flu of my own. I hadn't been as sick for years. Name the symptom: the chills, the sweats, the high fever. The list went on and on. Weakness, nausea, aches in every joint, the congestion, the cough that turned into bronchitis. On New Year's Eve, after spending most of the day in bed, I got up to feed Minnie and Harry but was back in bed by eight o'clock. I looked at myself in the mirror as I brushed my teeth. Scary. I was supposed to be on vacation through Sunday, January 8. Some vacation! I wondered how I would put away all the Christmas ornaments, drag the tree out to the street, pack, then haul my sick self and two dogs home to New York on the seventh. What would happen to my stuffed-up ears on the plane? Soon I would have more to worry about.

It was a day or so after the holiday, Tuesday or Wednesday, the third or fourth, that I got a call from my office informing me that once I was back, I would have a week to do a comprehensive story summing up the Obama administration, all eight years. It had to air on January 15, the Sunday before President Barack Obama left office. That meant studying the three-inch-thick research book that was overnighted to me, screening video of *all* the key moments during the Obama presidency, doing at least three interviews starting that coming Monday. With whom? Where? Details still being worked out. Writing the piece and putting it together would mean all-nighters, plural.

And then on Friday, January 6, just as I was trying to figure out how I'd get through the next week, I received an email. It was from my au pair, just a few sentences informing me that I would be as surprised as he was: he had moved in with his boyfriend. The keys to the apartment were on the kitchen counter. He thanked me for the opportunity to work for me.

I was stunned. I emailed him back and said I was happy for him, but customarily, employees give at least a two-week notice. Since I was going out of town as soon as I got home, and there had been no warning, perhaps he could help out for a few days until I found someone to fill in? I said it would take several weeks to find a replacement. No reply.

The au pairs who have cared for my dogs have been quite a group. Here's a partial list: an evangelist, who made money for her ministry in Uganda doing cabaret shows and reflexology, a form of foot massage somewhat related to acupuncture. A student from Belgrade, who earned a Ph.D. in biochemistry; she now works for a pharmaceutical company and lives in Switzerland. A multilingual German girl, who went on to become a flight attendant for British Airways and then an event planner. The daughter of Romanian diplomats, who is now an architect in charge of all the building projects for a hotel chain. A film school graduate, who collaborated with her father, the editor of a Lima newspaper, on a book about Peruvian food and has worked for the UN. A Japanese translator, whose mother made glorious sushi feasts when she came to visit and sometimes to substitute for her daughter. A student from the Ivory Coast, who took Piggy with her to French business classes at the Alliance Française in London. There have been at least a dozen others. I've loved the incredible variety of people who answered my ads and didn't think being a dog au pair was strange. Most of them have been interesting people. I suppose they would have to be a little unconventional to see the possibilities of the job. Some have stayed a few months, a year. Some have stayed four or five years and remain my friends. Typically, they're in their early to mid-twenties, just out of college or close to it, and are figuring out what to do with themselves. My home is a kind of halfway house for them, a bridge between school and Life. They have real responsibility, but the work isn't heavy lifting.

In thirty years of employing dog au pairs, I've only had to fire three. This was the first time anyone had ever walked out with no notice. He was twenty-two, an aspiring artist, talented and charming. His personal style was a tad flamboyant. He often wore makeup. Sometimes I would come home and find little drifts of glitter around the apartment. A few months before he left, he lucked into a modeling assignment for a major fashion designer. Walking through Times Square one day, I looked up, and there he was on a billboard twenty feet high. Soon he was apprenticing with a makeup artist he'd met on the shoot. I liked him. I had no inkling he'd just leave.

Maybe a minute after walking in the door of my New York apartment, maybe thirty seconds after taking off my coat, I headed for his room. He hadn't bothered to clean up after himself before moving out. I found dirty linens and towels wadded up and scattered around, whatever he didn't want. On the desk sat two large zipper-seal bags bulging with cosmetics, stuffed so full neither one would close. Foundation, a regular rainbow of eye shadow colors, face powder, brushes of all sizes and shapes, concealers, blushes, mascara in various shades, nail polish, exponentially more makeup than I've ever owned at one time. Why would a would-be makeup artist leave behind hundreds of dollars' worth of professional supplies?

Furious about what he'd done, I picked up the bags of makeup and marched them out to the garbage. I spent the rest of the day cleaning the au pair's room and bathroom, so that anyone who agreed to help me out wouldn't have to move into a mess. All I wanted to do was dose myself with Ny-Quil and sleep off my flu, but I had to get up at four-thirty the next morning and fly to Boston to interview a presidential historian, then fly home that night.

Stephen and another friend agreed to feed and let the dogs out while I was gone. By chance, the adult daughter of a former colleague needed a place to stay. I got through the week and started hunting for a new au pair. Everything finally seemed to be getting back under control, and then it wasn't.

Carol hadn't even been dead for six weeks. How could Harry have cancer? He'd only just arrived. He was content. It was as if he'd been waiting all his life to have Minnie bossing him around. Minnie and Harry. They were like a couple who'd been married fifty years. They stretched out on the floor next to each other, their sides touching, their paws intertwined. Harry had calmed down so much that Dr. Farber was cutting back on his antianxiety drugs. His colitis had disappeared.

And I loved him. Waiting for the biopsy results, I walked around whispering to myself, "Please don't die. Not now, not so soon. Minnie and I need you to be part of our little family."

Dr. Farber called me in the afternoon. Harry had something called a mast cell tumor, common in dogs. We scheduled surgery for the following Tuesday to remove it.

The good news: the surgery went well. Harry's cancer hadn't spread. The bad news: the tumor was of a type that was likely to recur. Next, to the oncologist. We decided the treatment that would be the most manageable, for Harry and for me, given my unpredictable travel schedule, was six months of an oral chemotherapy drug called Palladia, given at home every other day, along with a course of steroids. The cost was staggering, a thousand dollars a month, on top of thousands more I'd already paid for his vet visits, tests, and the surgery.

An oncology tech handed me a bottle of orange pills and a bag full of purple surgical gloves. "What are these for?" I pointed to the gloves. "Palladia is toxic to humans," she replied. "You can't allow the pills to touch your skin." And I was supposed to feed them to a dog? A frightening thought.

What kinds of side effects could I expect? "Diarrhea, nausea, lethargy, lameness." Poor Harry.

Just before Christmas, I'd learned I would be going to England on assignment toward the end of February. I decided I had to see the bathrooms Carol had designed for the Morgans hotel in London. I would be traveling around the country for ten days shooting three stories, with a Saturday free in London because we weren't able to arrange any of our interviews for that day. Perfect timing. I would take pictures in the ladies' room and send them to Carol's friends. Maybe, somehow, I'd be allowed into the men's room to take pictures there, too. I remembered the beautiful green rainforest world Carol had showed me on her computer, filled with birds and butterflies. The images were being laser-printed on tiles in Italy, she'd said.

I worried about the trip. The thought of leaving Harry concerned me. The oncologist reluctantly agreed to let me delay starting his chemo until I got home. I needed to observe him, I argued, to see whether he had any life-threatening side effects, to make sure there were no dosage mistakes, to get him to a vet if something went wrong. I couldn't pass off that responsibility to my temporary au pair. She was an adult, fifty years old, but it wasn't fair to expect her to react to an emergency if one occurred. I had hired a new, permanent au pair, but he wouldn't be moving in till I got back, so at least I wouldn't have to be concerned about leaving the dogs with someone who hadn't been trained.

Yes, I was anxious, but I was excited, too. I loved going to England. After living in London twice, for four years the first time, five years the second, it almost felt like home still. I would see friends, go to a play. Our shooting schedule was grueling, but so what? The stories were all great, *and* I would be able to see Carol's last project realized.

My free Saturday turned out to be cold, drizzly, and gray. It was lunchtime when I headed for St. Martin's Lane, near London's theater district. I squeezed past the

301

people lined up outside a trendy Indian restaurant. I had to tilt my umbrella every time I passed someone, the sidewalk was so narrow. I looked for the Morgans hotel. I walked the entire length of the street but saw no signs. I did it again. Still nothing. Could the revolving door I kept passing be the right place, the one with the eerie blue and green lighting? A new building on an old street. I went in. Yes, it was the St. Martins Lane Hotel, owned by the Morgans Hotel Group.

The lobby was dimly lit, smallish, with more colored lighting: shafts of blue, green, and yellow beaming down from the ceiling into gloom. The look was self-conscious, minimalist. Leaning against one wall, a huge framed mirror. Next to a pillar, giant chess pieces. Knee-high in front of a tufted, red velvet bench, the oddest drinks tables I'd ever seen . . . a row of gleaming gold molars.

The young woman at the check-in desk was as sleek and hip as the decor aspired to be. I asked her about the bathrooms. I told her they were designed by a friend, who had died. She looked puzzled but led me to the lobby ladies' room and pushed open the door. I saw four plain, painted walls, each one a different color. No tiles. No lacy ferns. No butterflies. No rain forest. The magical green fantasy I had seen on Carol's computer wasn't there.

"And what about the men's room?" I asked. "Same," I was told. "I have to get back to reception." The young woman let the door close. She looked at me as if I were crazy, maybe somebody who should be escorted out by security. I asked her whether she knew what had happened, why the tiles hadn't been installed. I told her about Carol again, in more detail. With chilly politeness, she said she had no idea what I was talking about. I asked to see the manager. "He's not here today. I can give you his email address."

I felt a profound sadness. I had come expecting to see something beautiful, something of Carol — if not her epitaph, a glorious last splash of her talent, left behind for good. Artists are their art. Carol's death seemed unfair, cruel to me, at that moment even more so. I rounded the revolving door, escaped the strange blue and green light, and only then started to cry.

I emailed the general manager. Two days later, he replied that the tiles were never made, that the company had chosen "another direction."

TWENTY-TWO:
ON BORROWED TIME

Not long after I got back from England, Stephen came over with one last load of bull-terrier-abilia. I didn't think it was possible there could be more. He produced a rather good watercolor portrait of Harry with his bowl, and a rather bad oil painting of Violet. There was a photograph of Harry relaxing on a couch and others of Violet smiling. In one she's wearing a tutu, obviously competing in a Halloween costume contest for dogs. In another, she's draped across Santa's lap with a big red bow tied under her chin.

Stephen handed me a folio bulging with things Carol had collected God knows where. A couple of old black-and-white photographs in wood frames of unidentified, long-dead bull terriers. Framed pages from antique dog books with illustrations of bull terriers as they looked in the nineteenth century. A brass bridle ornament for a horse with the head of a bull terrier on it. What was that about? Bull terrier memo pads, a tacky plastic bull terrier hanging from a key chain, a carved wooden bull terrier bookmark, a necklace with the name HARRY spelled out in black laser-cut letters hanging from a chain, broken between the *H* and the *A* and glued back together. Best of all, a bull terrier postage stamp from Karachay-Cherkessia, a small Russian republic in the Caucasus Mountains not far from the Black Sea.

Every time Stephen showed up with more of Carol's stuff, I was amazed all over again not only by how much of it she had squirreled away, but by what it all was. "Carol wanted me to have the painting of Harry," he said, "but I'm giving it to you on long-term loan. You should have it." I thanked him.

Each time he arrived, Harry went wild, jumping, wagging, licking. The two of them played on the floor. When Stephen finally got up, he said, "I have a confession. I never told Carol this, but I didn't really like Harry very much. Now I do. He was always driving me crazy with the bowl and balls, for hours sometimes, nonstop. Annoying. He seems so much calmer, less neurotic. And you know what? He's all that's left of Carol. I really miss her. He's kind of become Carol for me. Does that sound weird?"

"No, not weird. I understand. I really miss Carol, too, and whenever I look at Harry, I think of her. But for me, it's memory that keeps her alive. All of her things that I've got now, like Harry's biker jacket or the one with all the funny pins or her *Adirondack Days* book that Lissa gave me. They exist in her image. They look like her sense of humor." I thought, She touched them with her magic wand.

Every other day, I put on a pair of purple surgical gloves and gave Harry his Palladia pill. My au pair did it if I was out of town.

Harry handled his chemotherapy pretty well, but slowly, over six months, I realized in retrospect the treatment had taken its toll. Or maybe it was age catching up with him. He was happy with Minnie and me. That was obvious, but I wondered whether he missed Carol. I hardly noticed the change in him at first. He played with his bowl and balls less. He and Minnie didn't roughhouse as often. His hind legs seemed a little stiff sometimes. His cracked foot never got better. I stopped taking him to the farmers market. He had trouble walking that far.

But I loved petting him and caring for him

and giving him foolish nicknames. I probably shouldn't admit calling him Hairy Harry because he shed a lot. Maybe that's why Carol named him Harry in the first place. He never did learn to like the beach, but when I took him to South Carolina, I loved his delight in curling up in his own patch of sunlight on the deck. I loved feeling him against me in bed at night and listening to him snore soft dog snores. I loved looking in his serious, dark eyes. I loved seeing Minnie and Harry together, even their conspiratorial stares as they worked me over for treats, the expectation on their faces as they watched me cook dinner, the bull terrier stubbornness in their eyes when they didn't want to do what I wanted them to do. How many times had Carol warned me that when Harry was tired of walking, he would simply lie down, until I agreed to turn around and go home? I loved that about him too.

May 5, 2017, was Harry's twelfth birthday. I sang "Happy Birthday" to him and gave both dogs marrow bones and lots of treats. Harry's special present was a memory-foam bed like Minnie's with his name on it.

In mid-May, an envelope arrived from a law firm. Inside, I found a check for seven thousand dollars, money Carol wanted me to have to help pay for Harry's care. I was touched. Anything left over when Harry died, she instructed, should be given to the bull terrier welfare fund operated by the Bull Terrier Club of America. Left over, if only! I think I spent seven thousand dollars on Harry just getting his tumor diagnosed and removed. Then there was the cost of his chemotherapy, not to mention his other medical bills. I remembered Carol's email describing Harry as "a money pit." I'll say, but I didn't care. Her boy was my boy now.

When she'd told me she intended to leave me money, I said it wasn't necessary. She insisted, but I never believed it would happen. By the end of her life, she didn't have any to leave, only a pile of debts. The money for Harry, I learned, came from the 9/11 Victim Compensation Fund. They had finally approved her claims.

Before long, a year had passed since Harry came to stay. On Halloween, I dressed him in his unicorn costume and sent pictures to Stephen and Lissa. Lissa sent me back one of Annabelle in a *T. rex* costume, but her message was about Carol. "I think about her every day, and time hasn't lessened how much I still miss her." I hadn't stopped missing her either.

In mid-November, for the first time that fall, I dressed the dogs in their jackets to go out in the morning. A front had blown through overnight, driven by strong winds. It was bright and cold, the sky a dazzling, perfect blue, 9/11 blue, I caught myself thinking. As we set off for Chelsea Piers, I looked across the street toward Clement Clarke Moore Park. The parked cars were covered with ginkgo leaves, blankets of them on roofs and windshields, pools of them underfoot. They were tender still, green and yellow. On the sidewalk, alongside the wrought-iron fence, there were so many, and they were so deep, people stopped and looked down for a moment in wonder before sloshing through them noisily on their way to somewhere else.

It was at that same spot almost exactly a year before, according to my cell phone photo file, at seven A.M. on November 20, that I had tied the dogs to the fence, so I that I could photograph them standing on a carpet of color, yellow and red trees tall behind them. I sent the picture to Carol, my attempt to give her one last autumn, even if she couldn't touch or smell it.

I wanted more than anything else to do it again, to photograph these new ginkgo leaves, freshly fallen and beautiful, before they were trampled and flattened, but after Carol died, I stopped taking my phone with me on walks. There seemed to be no need.

I can't remember now exactly when it was, but around that same time, Harry was diagnosed with kidney disease. He was lethargic, had lost weight, and was drinking too much water. Dr. Farber changed his diet to new and different kinds of prescription dog food. Kidney disease, ultimately, is fatal, but can, in some cases, be managed for years. I told myself Harry would be one of those cases. He liked his new food. I cupped some in my hands for him to try. He ate it all and licked my fingers till they were slimy. He regained the weight he'd lost and began acting like himself again, although his hind legs had been getting stiffer over the last few months. He needed help climbing stairs and sometimes had trouble getting to his feet on hardwood floors.

In South Carolina, a few days after Christmas, it was warm. I left the back doors open so the dogs could go out on the porch or down to the deck. I knew Harry would sun himself. Suddenly, I heard loud, frantic barking. Minnie. Then her little legs scrambling up the stairs to the porch. More barking. I wondered what her problem was. The door was open. She could get in. Something had to be wrong. When I reached the porch door, she was waiting for me, barking so hard her whole body shook. As soon as she saw me, she turned and raced back outside. I followed and saw Harry sprawled spread-eagle on the bottom two steps, looking up at me terrified, unable to move. It took all my strength to lift him to his feet and help him up the stairs into the house.

"Oh, Harry, Harry, please stay with us," I whispered into his fur as I hugged him. Minnie was at his side, concern on her face and in her body language. I'm sure I'll be accused of anthropomorphizing, but I simply can't buy the idea that dogs don't have the kinds of feelings humans do. Minnie saw that Harry was in trouble. She came to me and demanded I rescue him. There is no other explanation. When Harry met Minnie, they loved each other.

I brought the dogs back to New York in early January. On Monday, February 26, 2018, after a terrible, sleepless weekend, I had Harry put down. By then, he couldn't stand. He couldn't walk. He was in terrible pain.

I watched him crash. Hour by hour, he seemed to lose strength. And naturally, it rained, just as it had when Carol was dying. Rained and rained from Saturday afternoon till Monday morning, a cold, constant, hard rain. Harry couldn't hold still. He fussed and kept trying to reposition himself. To get him outside, I had to lift him up, carry him down the front stairs, and steady him on the sidewalk. His hind legs buckled when he tried to pee. We got soaked. On Saturday night, I boosted him into bed beside me. I couldn't sleep as he thrashed and turned, unable to settle in one spot. Around midnight, he heaved himself around and fell to the floor, landing with a thud. I rushed to him and held him as he panted, his distress and my anguish equal, there in the darkness. I let him rest. Eventually, arms under his belly, I managed to move him to the dog cushion at the foot of my bed, where his giraffe rug, the one that had traveled back and forth with him between Carol's apartment and mine, was spread out. I brought him a bowl of water and held it close to his mouth, so he could drink. At two-thirty, he seemed to want to go out. I held an umbrella over him. When we did it again at three-thirty, he collapsed in a muddy puddle.

By Sunday night, I was using a bath towel as a sling to stand him up and support his back legs. Why, why was this happening when I had to travel for work within hours, to the Florida Keys on Monday, back late Tuesday night, to Oakland, California early Wednesday morning through Friday? So far away. I wanted more than anything to stay home, to be with Harry, but I doubted anyone would understand if I backed out of a story at the last minute because of a dog. For a child, a spouse, a parent, maybe, but not a pet, no matter what that pet meant to me.

All weekend I tortured myself. Should I take Harry to the twenty-four-hour emergency vet, the specialty-care facility where his oncologist was? How would I get him there? Car services for pets don't come on short notice. They have to be scheduled. I had learned the hard way, on a previous occasion, that the emergency vet didn't have the ability to run more than routine tests on weekends or at night. No one would be able to do much of anything until Monday, when I had to go out of town. I knew I could leave him there. He might get something for his pain, but was I just prolonging his agony? What if he got worse? What if Harry died, alone? I couldn't bear that. He had slipped so much in just a few hours.

I got down on the floor and stretched out beside him. With my arms around him, I could feel him tremble. As I held him, I heard myself keening, moaning. I couldn't stop the sound. I thought about Carol. What would she do? What would she want me to do? Our poor Harry. Was it fair to let him go on suffering? Had he lost his dignity? And what about his kidney disease? Lying there on the floor, I decided that I would take him to Dr. Farber. He had known Harry since he was a puppy. He'd known Carol. He knew me. I would ask him what he thought, whether he could save Harry. "Please, say yes," I said into Harry's fur. I would hear Dr. Farber out, but deep down I knew what was going to happen.

I remembered the extra pain pills Harry hadn't needed after his cancer surgery, angry at myself that I hadn't thought of them earlier. I gave him one. For the first time in two days, he relaxed and slept. I didn't. I listened to him breathe. I listened to the rain, sick inside that I knew what Harry did not, that this would, probably, be the last night of his life.

In the morning, I made breakfast for Minnie *and* Harry. The irony didn't escape me that I was feeding a dog who would most likely be dead in what, three hours? I said to myself, "I can't let him die hungry," and then, "But maybe he has a chance." I took him to Dr. Farber. He said it was possible that Harry had a tumor on his spine or that he had the equivalent of a bad back. "Even if his cancer hasn't spread, he could be like this for months and in pain."

I asked what he thought, whether it was time. "Yes." I told him I couldn't watch Harry suffer. He said, "I'll give you as long as you need alone with him." The hardest part of my decision was knowing that I was making it for Carol, too. Would she agree it was time? Did she want him back?

Nobody ever says anything, but when it's likely that your pet will be put down, the vet techs take you to an exam room away from the others, to the one with a stainless steel platform that can be raised or lowered. They'd put a blanket on the platform for Harry and set the height so I could sit with him.

One of the receptionists came in the room with forms to sign or something. I don't remember why he was there. I looked up. "Will you do me a favor?" I asked. "I don't have any pictures of me with Harry. Could you please take some?" Unspoken between us, the words *before it's too late.* I handed him my cell phone, and we posed for the camera, Harry and I, our heads together. Hairy Harry, Handsome Harry, Harry the Ham till the end. Sometimes I can't look at those pictures. There are eight of them.

I held Harry in my arms, my face against his, for ten minutes, fifteen, I don't know, talking to him, saying how much I loved him, kissing him, before Dr. Farber came back with two syringes, the first injection to sedate him, the second to stop his heart. When his head drooped, I said goodbye, told him that wherever she was, Carol needed him, and started to cry.

I took Harry's collars and his red bootie with me when I walked home. I sat with Minnie for half an hour. Oh, Minnie. I wondered whether she understood. She saw me take him away. How would she endure losing him? I wondered. How would I? I hugged her as hard as I could for as long as I could until the car service came to take me to the airport. On the plane, I tried to hide my face, so that no one would notice I couldn't stop crying. Driving from Miami to Key Largo with a colleague, it was harder. At least she was driving, looking straight ahead at the road, not at me.

The next day, we were shooting at a dolphin sanctuary for a story on animal intelligence. I interviewed a scientist about identifying the unique whistles these mammals use to communicate, but what viewers commented on was the end of the piece, when two lovely, shiny dolphins rose out of the water together and gave me a kiss as I knelt on the dock. It's a trick they've been trained to perform on command. My colleagues thought the whole stunt was "a hoot, so fun," but being touched by an animal made my sadness bearable. Two days later, in California, at the Oakland Zoo, Donna, the elephant, who can look at a picture of a banana and then point to the real thing, caressed me with her trunk.

Every day, Minnie smelled Harry's giraffe rug all over, as if she were checking to see whether he'd come home. She refused to set foot on his memory-foam bed, walked around it to get up on the couch in the den, and wouldn't go for walks. Finally, in the spring, she consented to come with me to the farmers market again.

TWENTY-THREE:
WHAT WOULD CAROL
HAVE THOUGHT?

To say that the first attempt to scatter Carol's ashes didn't go well would be an understatement. It was a disaster.

What cascaded into catastrophe began with minor complications, such as, who actually had Carol's ashes? I didn't know. Stephen didn't either, but he figured he could find out easily enough. Carol died in December 2016. More than a year later, the matter of where her ashes would be scattered and when had fallen off her friends' radar. At first they talked about it a lot, swore she had disclosed to each of them what she wanted. After all, she planned her own memorial, every last detail, including who would speak. It took place at the end of May, nearly six months after her death. I was out of town, so couldn't go, but was given a stack of the programs. Carol's friend Michael Boodro, then editor of *Elle Decor,* and his husband, Robert Pini, put the program together, eight and a half by eleven inches, glossy and stiff, the cover lipstick red, with a perfectly composed photo of a young Carol in profile on it, her hair dark then, pinned up. She was wearing sunglasses and was artfully holding a large coffee cup in her manicured fingers. The caption said *Carol Fertig, a Life of Passion and Style.* Inside there was a whole page of pictures: Carol young and old, with her friends, with her cat, Bruno, photos of Violet, of people and objects she admired, opposite a tribute Boodro and Pini wrote. "A relationship with Carol was a fantastic, gloriously luscious, and baroque experience," it began. On the back, Carol's favorite picture of herself with Harry, the one where she's wearing her fur hat with earflaps, and Harry's bowl and balls are parked beside her on a bench. The memorial took place at the venue she chose, overlooking the Hudson River, not far from where the Staten Island ferry docks, renewing speculation about what she wanted done with her ashes.

Definitely, the Hudson River by Battery Park. From a boat. No, in the Adirondacks at the Lake Placid Lodge. Some in each place. Her friends, I was told, discussed the matter and then went on their way, resolving nothing. Without Carol, they didn't see each other much anymore and seldom talked.

So time passed and then more time before Stephen brought it up again the following spring. He said he definitely remembered her mentioning the Hudson River. The Adirondacks would be nice, he said, but expensive and difficult to schedule. "Getting Carol's friends together will be hard enough in New York, let alone there."

So, the two of us made the decision. The Hudson River it would be, on a Sunday afternoon. Soon, we hoped. Stephen, as one of Carol's executors, had a list of email addresses and offered to contact everybody on it to find out when they'd be in town. "Summer can be tricky."

That it was. Alan Wade was headed to Europe, Ann King to Mexico, where her daughter lives. Mary Corliss also had a big trip coming up, her first since her husband died. Several people didn't reply. Stephen was sorry he'd ever gotten involved by the time June 24 was determined to be the best possible day for everybody, the only day for some.

It was also the day two million people descended on New York City for the annual Gay Pride March. Two million on top of the millions already here. The city swarming with dancing revelers carrying signs and rainbow banners, many in elaborate costumes, spilling out of restaurants and bars. Those descriptions of groups: a pride of lions, a flock of geese, et cetera, on June 24, Manhattan would host a pandemonium of people. It would be traffic hell.

We checked the route and timing of the parade. A noon start at Sixteenth Street, south on Seventh Avenue, east to Fifth Avenue, then north to Twenty-ninth Street. The opposite direction from where we intended to be. Supposedly no street closures anywhere near us. Good. If we said sunset in Battery Park, the southern tip of Manhattan, surely, we thought, we'd be okay. By then, the event would be over, the marchers and bystanders dispersed, the traffic gone.

The days were long. Sunset on June 24 would be at 8:31 P.M. Assuming good weather, we decided to gather at seven next to the Staten Island ferry dock, scatter the ashes, then regroup at a picnic table or a bench for a toast. Ann King offered to bring wine and cheese. In case of rain, the plan was to go ahead anyway and find a restaurant or bar where we could have our toast inside.

Stephen discovered that Jeffrey Mendoza,

321

Carol's friend the landscape designer, had her ashes. He and his partner, Chuck Sklar, the children's endocrinologist at Sloan Kettering, who had been at Carol's side when she died, couldn't attend, so Stephen collected the urn well in advance. I had Harry's ashes and those of her cat, Bruno.

"We can mix them together," Stephen suggested. "The container from the crematorium is really ugly. So are the ones Harry and Bruno are in." I'd shown him the plain wooden boxes. "Carol would be horrified. She would expect to go out in style," he said, chuckling over the phone. "I have a collection of really pretty small baskets and lacquer boxes. And antique, carved scoops. Some are bone. Some are wood. I have silver ones as well." Stephen, the architect, designing a beautiful way to do a sad thing. "I'll come over early, before we go to Battery Park. We can divide up the ashes, so everybody has some to scatter."

"I want to keep half of Harry's," I said. "He was my dog, too. I told you about the little shrine I have in my closet where I keep Piggy's ashes and Goose's. When I die, I want them buried with me. Minnie's, too."

"What time should I come by?"

Knowing Stephen was always late, I said, "Before five. We'll need time to get everything ready."

What could go wrong?

Plenty.

On Sunday, five o'clock came and went. No Stephen. Needless to say. Five-fifteen. Five-thirty. Still no Stephen. I began to get nervous. At about five forty-five, my phone rang. Stephen.

"Bring some ID to the corner, something that shows you live on the block, so I can get the cop to let me turn onto Twenty-second Street."

"What?" I had no idea what he was talking about.

"Your street is closed. I told the cop I needed to park by your place because I had to bring in the ashes and all the other stuff. He won't let me."

Stephen sounded agitated. I could tell because his voice tends to get higher when he's worked up. I remembered all those calls from his car and the night Carol died.

"Okay, I'll be right there. I'll look for a utility bill or something." I rummaged around and found one, grabbed my passport, phone, and keys, then headed down the street. I could see bumper-to-bumper traffic on Tenth Avenue, going nowhere. There was a barrier at my corner. I wondered why. The Gay Pride parade was over.

The published list of street closures hadn't included my neighborhood. I'd been indoors most of the afternoon. What on earth was going on?

I spotted Stephen, practically belly to chest with a much-taller cop, the two of them silhouetted in the late-afternoon sun, their body language confrontational. Uh-oh. When I reached them, I said, "Officer, here's my identification and a utility bill to show I live on this block, so that you can let my friend bring his car in." The cop, who had been ranting at Stephen, while he ranted back, turned in my direction. A good-looking guy in his twenties, he had lots of thick dark hair. He was bright red, bust-a-gasket red, and sweating.

"He ran over me and left me to die!"

I wasn't sure I heard right. "Officer, here's my passport and a utility bill to show you that I live on this block. This is a friend of mine. We're supposed to be scattering someone's ashes this evening, someone dear to both of us. We need to transport the urn and other things, and they're heavy. He needs to get to my house, so we can do that. Could he please drive his car as far as my building?"

"He ran over me and left me to die," the

cop bleated again, looking as if he might cry.

"Excuse me, I don't understand." He was very much alive, his uniform crisp and fresh.

"He defied my order to stop. He ran over me. My foot."

Stephen: "I was trying to park. You . . . you . . . jumped in front of my car."

The cop: "You disobeyed my order. My foot. My foot is crushed. You tried to kill me."

I looked down at his feet. He had a dusty scuff mark on the toe of one of his black boots, no indentation, just a scuff. I had just seen him walk, perfectly normally, without so much as a hint of a limp.

Stephen: "I did not try to kill you. When I tried to turn out of traffic, you jumped in front of my car." Stephen had reached full tenor. The cop was borderline hysterical, his voice even higher than Stephen's. I looked around and noticed that a couple of other officers, who had been standing on the far side of Tenth Avenue, had edged in closer. A crowd of gawkers had appeared. I heard a siren getting louder. A patrol car was nudging its way through the traffic on Tenth. It reached the corner and stopped. Someone dragged the barrier aside and it turned onto Twenty-second Street. Two officers got out and approached.

Stephen and I tried to tell the two officers that we needed their help, but they had come to execute some sort of divide-and-conquer play. One positioned his body between us and the cop who had confronted Stephen. The other took the cop by the arm, supporting him as he hobbled toward the patrol car, limping badly all of a sudden. With each step, he winced and groaned. I couldn't believe it.

Instead of allowing us to explain, the other half of the divide-and-conquer team demanded our names, addresses, and telephone numbers and walked off, leaving us standing by ourselves in the street.

More police arrived and a big red SUV, a fire emergency-medical vehicle. Two EMTs rushed to the patrol car where Officer Left-to-Die was now sitting sideways in the back seat with his legs sticking out of the open door. They leaned over his supposedly crushed foot. I watched them take off his boot and sock, then bend his ankle and bare toes.

I looked around and saw my neighbors staring, gossiping among themselves, a few pointing. I felt like an animal in a circus. On the periphery of this gathering stood a stone-faced, older police officer in the cleanest, stiffest, whitest white shirt I think I've ever seen, not a wrinkle anywhere. Appearing to give orders to the two younger officers at his side, he had rank written all over him.

I called Ann King and told her what was happening. She lived around the corner on Twenty-third Street and soon joined us, carrying a canvas bag containing what was supposed to be the wine and hors d'oeuvres for our toast. I asked her to phone the other people who were supposed to scatter Carol's ashes and to suggest we all meet at my apartment instead of Battery Park. I gave her my keys, so she could let them in.

Next, an ambulance showed up, lights flashing, siren blaring. With amazing speed, doors opened, a stretcher appeared, and Officer Left-to-Die was lifted onto it. He was bundled into the back and rushed to a hospital. I heard a couple of New York cynics muttering, "Eh, he figures he'll have a pension for life, that guy" and "He's got it made now."

The show goes on, I thought, and began counting uniforms. Seventeen. Fifteen cops, most of whom were by then chatting with one another and laughing, plus the two fire department EMTs, who were filling out some sort of forms inside the red SUV.

Seventeen! I marveled. All this because Stephen got himself into an argument over turning onto my street. Only in New York.

More than an hour into this little drama, Stephen's battered Land Rover was still stopped at the intersection, still holding up traffic on Tenth Avenue. The front tires were turned to the right, toward the barrier now blocking Twenty-second Street again. I watched a police photographer take pictures. Other officers looked up at light poles and the stoplight checking for security cameras.

Stephen and I began talking to two relaxed, seen-it-all guys, who said they were from the Tenth Precinct, the jurisdiction in charge of policing my neighborhood. They were the only officers who seemed willing to listen. Just then, another divide-and-conquer team moved in. "Sir, could you please come with us for a moment," they asked, but didn't give Stephen the option to say no. He looked back at me, confused, as they pushed him toward the fence at Clement Clarke Moore Park. I continued talking with the two men from the Tenth Precinct.

"I'm a reporter," I said, and identified myself. "I've covered police activity of one kind or another for more than forty years, but I've never seen anything quite like this."

"We tried to step in," one of them replied. "We were prepared to give your friend a warning and just let it go at that, but it was taken out of our hands. Somebody complained up the chain of command." He nodded at the stern officer in the very white shirt. "What you don't know is that this is tangled up in a turf battle. The guy who went to the hospital, he isn't an actual cop. He's a civilian traffic enforcement agent." The other one went on, "They're not really trained. We have problems with them all the time. But the Traffic division protects them."

Out of the corner of my eye, I saw activity where Stephen stood surrounded. His arms were behind his back. A cop was pulling plastic ties tight around his wrists.

"What's happening?" I asked, dumbfounded.

The Tenth Precinct guys glanced over. "I guess we're gonna have to take him in. Don't worry, it'll just be like someone getting arrested at a demonstration. He'll be out in an hour, an hour and a half. It's nothing, a misdemeanor. Won't even go on his record."

Stephen was walked to the Tenth Precinct car and maneuvered into the back seat the way suspects are in television shows, with a hand on his head.

"Do you drive?" The officer who had re-assured me held up Stephen's keys.

"Yes."

"Here." He handed them to me and asked me to sign a receipt. "Someone will call you in a little while. If you haven't heard from us by eight-thirty, give the precinct a call."

Car doors slammed, and Stephen was driven away. The crowd drifted off. The street was opened to traffic, the barrier moved aside. Where had all the cops gone? It was as if they had evaporated.

I was standing alone next to Stephen's car, now double-parked on Twenty-second Street. I got in. The front seat was pulled so far forward, the steering wheel was practically against my chest. I couldn't figure out how to move it back. I also couldn't find the switch for the dome light or the air-conditioning dials or the lights or anything else it normally takes thirty seconds to locate in a rental car. I did find the ignition, though, and managed, by some miracle, to get the thing into a parking spot in front of my building. Unfortunately, I couldn't make the windows close, so they stayed open. I hoped nobody would break in.

A wire-mesh bin was sitting on the pas-senger seat, in it, lovely boxes. A woven wicker one had a cutout photo of Carol as a young woman stuck to it. Another box, made out of some exotic streaked wood, had a card attached with a gold, embossed bull terrier on it. Harry's name was hand-printed in calligraphy. A third looked like a little trunk with brass findings. Bruno was printed on a hand-colored picture of a tiger. There were scoops, and Stephen's straw hat.

By the time I carried the bin into my apartment, Ann King had opened the wine she'd brought and found glasses in my kitchen. Mary Corliss and Alan Wade were there, too. We were all too shocked to say much. We waited. No one called.

At eight-thirty, I phoned the Tenth Precinct and asked the duty officer about Stephen, when he'd be released.

"Oh, the Felony Assault with Grievous Bodily Harm guy. He's not getting out."

"What? *Felony?* You must have him mixed up with somebody else. The officers who took him away said he'd be released in an hour or an hour and a half."

"No, he's going to be transported downtown to One Hundred Centre Street to be charged."

"Could I please speak with one of the officers who brought him in?"

"I'll have him call you." He took my phone number and hung up.

Ann, Alan, and Mary stared at me. We kept repeating the word *felony*, trying to comprehend.

"Why One Hundred Centre Street?" I asked. I remembered the tall gray building all the way downtown where I'd had to report for jury duty several times.

"It's the criminal courts building," Alan said.

The phone rang.

It was Stephen. "The Tenth Precinct officer was really nice and gave my phone back to call you. He wasn't supposed to." All of Stephen's personal possessions had been confiscated when he arrived at the station.

"What's going on?" I sounded frantic even to myself. "The guy at the desk told me you were being charged with felony assault. That's serious."

"Yeah. Because I supposedly injured a cop. Aggravated assault with grievous bodily harm. They're transporting me down to One Hundred Centre Street and putting me in the jail in the basement till I'm charged, probably not till tomorrow morning."

"Jail!" I was practically shouting. Then the practical side of me took over. "I have an early assignment tomorrow, so I'll give your car keys to Ann King. Contact her when you get out. What about Wally? Is there

somebody who can take care of him?"

Stephen's beautiful old golden retriever, Teddy, had died. Now he had a puppy, named Wally.

"My neighbor." He gave me his neighbor's phone number. "Tell her that there's a spare key hidden in the fuse box opposite my front door. Wally plays with her dog all the time."

I grabbed my second cell phone. "Stay on the line. Let me call her, in case she's not home, and we have to come up with somebody else."

I dialed the number. His neighbor answered. Startled, she couldn't quite take in what I was telling her. "Hello, my name is Martha Teichner."

"Who?"

"I'm calling on behalf of Stephen Miller Siegel, who is about to go to jail and desperately needs you to take care of Wally." I realized I sounded like one of those Nigerian money scammers, minus the money part. Why would she believe me? "He's on the phone in my other ear. I need to make sure you have Wally before the police make him hang up."

I heard her moving, rummaging around, turning the knob on a lock. Hallelujah!

"I'm going out the door. . . . I'm opening

the fuse box. . . . Yup, here it is. . . . I'm going into Stephen's apartment now." Thumping noise. "I've got Wally. He'll be fine."

To Stephen, "Is there anybody else I need to call? Do you have a lawyer?"

"No, the only lawyer I've ever dealt with is a real estate guy, who negotiated a lease for office space. Oh, and the lawyer who did Carol's will." I heard another voice. Stephen said, "I've got to go."

Alan, Ann, Mary, and I looked up the penalty for conviction on charges of aggravated assault against a police officer. Up to fifteen years in prison. We stared at each other incredulous.

Then somebody said, "I'm hungry." We were all hungry. It was nine-thirty by then. We walked around the corner to a little Italian restaurant directly across Tenth Avenue from the spot where Stephen's confrontation had occurred. We settled in for our meal and some red wine. We relaxed and laughed, but from time to time confessed to feeling guilty that we were enjoying ourselves while Stephen was in jail.

On our way back to my apartment, I asked, "What would Carol have thought?"

Ann and Alan laughed. Both said at once, "She would have thought the whole thing was hilarious."

■ ■ ■ ■

Stephen was charged and then released in the morning. He was assigned a court-appointed attorney. A court date was set. His personal effects were still at the Tenth Precinct, so he had to go there and collect them. The officer who allowed him call me also let him keep the money he had in his pocket, so at least he was able to get a cab back to the station.

When I spoke to him, he sounded cheerful, to my amazement. "It was an interesting experience."

"And that's a euphemism for what?" I asked, but there was no sarcasm at all in his account of his night in jail.

"They took me in through the loading dock in back of the building, where all the garbage cans are, and then down into the basement. The company was pretty congenial. There were a bunch of us all in the same cell. Nobody could sleep. They brought us some food, but it looked really bad, so I didn't eat it. I was starving when I got out. The worst thing was that the air-conditioning was so cold I could barely stand it."

"Were you scared?"

335

"No, not really. There were some drunks and some guys in there for robbery and drugs. There was a transvestite, who'd been in the Gay Pride March. Somebody stole her wig, a really expensive wig, so she ran after him and smashed right into a cop by mistake. That's why she was arrested. There was a kind of gallows humor. I was the only white person."

"What about the lawyer?"

"I liked him. He couldn't believe the charge and said not to worry, he would get it knocked down."

Sure enough, when investigators reviewed the various security-camera views of the scene, and Officer Left-to-Die's medical report came back with no grievous bodily harm evident, the charge was reduced to a misdemeanor. Just as the officers from the Tenth Precinct had predicted, like a nonviolent demonstrator arrested at a protest. Stephen pleaded guilty. He was fined $250 and sentenced to attend a one-week anger-management class.

A farce, yes, and given the outcome, pretty funny after all.

For weeks, Carol's ashes sat on my dining table in their woven wicker box, the cutout photograph of her face smiling up at me every time I passed by, her hair still dark in the picture, her lipstick very red, a hand posed against her cheek, like a glove model in a 1950s magazine. The wire-mesh bin with Stephen's boxes and scoops remained exactly where I'd left them the night he went to jail.

We decided to try again to scatter the ashes. Stephen emailed Carol's friends. Nobody was available for months.

"Let's do it anyway," Stephen said. "Soon. Let's not wait."

On the afternoon of August 12, watching Stephen remove Carol's picture from the top of her box, I felt strange, lightheaded, as if I were trespassing in a sacred place. We opened it and took out the plastic bag containing her ashes. I added half of Harry's and all of Bruno's and mixed them around with one of the scoops. I held open a zipper bag and Stephen poured. A dusty cloud rose around the opening. When we each had approximately equal amounts, he closed his bag and replaced its wire tie, exactly the same kind people use when they measure out bags of bulk nuts at the supermarket. Plastic bags and wire ties. I expected something more reverential, less expedient, less throwaway.

Stephen put his bag back in the wicker

box and replaced Carol's picture. He put my bag in the shiny box made out of streaked wood and slipped the latch closed.

"Should we see if Minnie is willing to come along?" I asked. "She deserves to be there," Stephen answered.

Minnie took some convincing. She balked at first, locking her legs so that a tug on her leash meant all four feet skidded along the sidewalk. She gave me that bull terrier look, sullen and stubborn and sly. The standoff lasted several minutes before she reconsidered her resistance and started walking. I had a bag of treats in my pocket to encourage her to keep going. Stephen carried the bin with the containers of ashes and two scoops.

At six P.M., the park at Chelsea Piers was crawling with people, nothing like the quiet, contemplative place it was at dawn, when I normally went there. I was surprised, but I shouldn't have been. It was Sunday, hot and bright, a little windy.

We had to navigate the cyclists and skateboarders, the food vendors and runners and slow-strolling families admiring megayachts moored along the piers for the summer. The benches were crowded with couples sitting close together, their arms around each other, with smokers and people eating and homeless men stretched out sleeping. Tourists were taking pictures of themselves at a spot where way in the distance they could see the Statue of Liberty. As if Lady Liberty might actually show up in their selfies.

I tied Minnie's leash to an empty picnic table nearby. Stephen set down the bin. Between us and the Hudson River, a waist-high railing overlooked a ledge wide enough to stand on, bolted to huge wooden pilings. The water was a good eight feet below us. We were as close as we could get to it. The logistics of ash scattering here were obvious. Who hasn't heard stories of people emptying out urns only to have the ashes blow back all over them, in their eyes, on their clothes? The stories are told as jokes. Ha-ha funny, unless it happens to you. We tried to figure out the wind direction.

As we took out our scoops and opened the two boxes, I wondered whether anybody would ask what we were doing or whether it was legal. People were all around us. We must have looked a little odd, but no one paid any attention. This was New York, after all.

"Okay, this is it," Stephen said as he dug into his bag of ashes. I held off, considering where to stand and how to aim. Stephen tossed his first scoopful as far over the railing as he could reach. Gray powder fell on the ledge. He tried again. Same result. He grabbed the plastic bag, bent down, pushed his head and shoulders through the rails, and shook the ashes into the water. The wind caught the gray cloud, and it, too, settled on the ledge.

"Damn!" Stephen climbed all the way through the railing, stood on the ledge, and tried to sweep the ashes into the river with his feet. By this time, we were both laughing. I got out my cell phone and began shooting video of his peculiar shuffle.

"I can't believe you're taking pictures of this. It's sooo disrespectful," Stephen said sarcastically, and laughed some more. He went back to his footwork for another minute or so and then stopped. I stopped shooting. We looked at each other and then at the river and didn't say a word. Neither one of us cried as it hit us both that we were there to say goodbye.

But goodbye to what? To Carol and Harry and Bruno? To their remains? Sacks of ashes were not what remained of them. They left behind memories. Memories are our true remains, to be treasured, to be shared, to dim, and eventually to be lost, when no one is left to remember. So why was it hard to let go, to part with those ashes? What were we afraid of losing? I don't know the answer.

I decided to write this book because I didn't want to stop living the story of what happened when Harry met Minnie. I didn't want to forget any of it, even the sad parts. This story of unexpected friendship, of love, was a wonderful gift, and in the end it made me and Minnie happy.

Harry did love Minnie, and she loved him. He was like a guest, fashionable, with impeccable manners, who arrived with a lot of luggage and some complicated dietary needs, but filled our hearts and left too soon. Minnie misses him. So do I.

And I will always miss Carol. When I think of her, I imagine a shower of confetti, big, colorful squares of it fluttering down around me, gold and silver ones among them, adding pizzazz, catching the light.

Stephen broke the silence. "Your turn." I climbed through the railing, crouched on the ledge, and just for a few seconds hesitated before emptying scoops of ashes into the Hudson. I expected them to disappear instantly, to dissolve, but they didn't. The river water wasn't clear, but it was clear enough so that for a while I could see circles of gray, lingering in layers a few inches down, sinking slowly, something so final in the way they faded away.

When I couldn't see them anymore, I whispered, "Thank you, Carol. Thank you, Harry."

ACKNOWLEDGMENTS

So many people to thank . . . I have to begin with Carol.

I thank Carol for bequeathing me so much more than her dog and for trusting me to find something other than just sadness in the last months of her life. She was big-hearted and generous with her friendship and with her friends, who made a place for me, when they could have treated the stranger in their midst as an intruder. I'm especially grateful to Stephen and Lissa.

And speaking of friends, thank you to my friend Reggie Nadelson, a terrific writer, who heard what I was writing about and insisted that I meet her agent, William Clark. I'd never written a book before. I didn't even know there was such a thing as a book proposal. William showed me a few proposals for books he'd sold, including one of Reggie's. He was the perfect teacher and a patient man, seeing me through the six months it took to write my own, then critiquing it and making suggestions . . . gently. He sent it out on a Monday. By Friday we had multiple offers. I couldn't believe it.

I chose Celadon Books because, from the very beginning, Jamie Raab, Celadon's president and publisher, got *When Harry Met Minnie.* I wanted her to be the editor. I knew that my story and I would come out whole at the end of the process and would be better for it. As a first-time author, I felt safe, not scared. I also want to thank Randi Kramer, Jamie's capable assistant, for all her help. Without Randi, I would have disappeared in technological quicksand.

Which brings me to the audiobook version of *When Harry Met Minnie.* Thank you to Mary Beth Roche at Macmillan Audio for loving Harry and Minnie even though she doesn't love dogs and for indulging me when I said I wanted to record the book myself, to tell my own story. I am very grateful to Matie Argiropoulos and Katherine Cook, who gently nudged me through a very strenuous four days by tantalizing me with descriptions of the fabulous lunches they would order in. Because of coronavirus, Matie had to direct remotely from her apartment in Brooklyn, but we actually met, fittingly, at the Union Square farmers market. I could at least see Katherine, through a window, wearing her mask as she recorded me at CDM Sound Studios in Manhattan. I never laid eyes on Chris Howerton but offer him my sympathy and my thanks for putting all my stops and starts together and making them sound like a real audiobook.

And many thanks to Kate Adams and her colleagues at Aster for deciding that Harry and Minnie's story should be told in the UK and beyond.

As the deadline to deliver the first draft of my manuscript approached, I decided to take a couple of weeks of vacation to finish it. On the Friday before taking the time off, I discovered that my new downstairs neighbor was about to begin major construction in her apartment, directly under my dining table, where I had written most of the book. Frantic, I tried to figure out where I could find a quiet place to work. I remembered the New York Public Library, the very first place I ever visited in New York City more than fifty years ago, while I was in college. I think I was nineteen. My flights home for Christmas had been canceled because of a blizzard. I ended up stranded at La Guardia Airport with time on my hands. A Harvard student, who was also stranded, suggested we go into the city. He'd been there before. I hadn't, so he offered to be my guide. He took me straight to the library on Fifth Avenue. It looked like a palace. We trudged through deep snow up unshoveled steps, between Patience and Fortitude, the library's famous marble lions, at that moment wearing what looked like comical snow hats. Walking into the spectacular main reading room was thrilling.

I knew that many books had been written in that wonderful building, but I also knew that it could take months for a workspace to open up. I called anyway. It was four P.M. on a Friday. Zero chance anybody would even call me back, I thought. Well, I was wrong. Within three hours Melanie Locay, from the Center for Research in the Humanities, had not only called but had arranged to meet me the following Monday morning to show me the small, snug Shoichi Noma Reading Room and give me a card key so that I could come and go as I pleased. She told me her mother was a big fan of *CBS Sunday Morning* and that she was excited to meet me. I could hardly contain MY excitement meeting HER. Thank you Melanie, more than you know. I loved listening to the echo as I walked the library's grand halls. I loved stealing glances at the two or three other people I'd see working nearby every day and wondered who they were and what they were writing. I loved sitting in my heavy oak chair reliving what happened when Harry met Minnie. I thought to myself: Imagine me writing a book and doing it at the New York Public Library. What could be better than that!

ABOUT THE AUTHOR

Martha Teichner has been a correspondent for "CBS Sunday Morning" since December 1993, where she's equally adept at covering major breaking national and international news stories as she is handling in-depth cultural and arts topics. Since joining CBS News in 1977, Teichner has earned multiple national awards for her original reporting, including 11 Emmy Awards and five James Beard Foundation Awards. Teichner was also part of the team coverage of the Newtown, Conn., elementary school shooting, which earned CBS News a 2014 duPont-Columbia Award. Teichner was born in Traverse City, Mich. She graduated from Wellesley College in 1969 with a bachelor's degree in economics. She attended the University of Chicago's Graduate School of Business Administration. Teichner resides in New York City.

The employees of Thorndike Press hope you have enjoyed this Large Print book. All our Thorndike, Wheeler, and Kennebec Large Print titles are designed for easy reading, and all our books are made to last. Other Thorndike Press Large Print books are available at your library, through selected bookstores, or directly from us.

For information about titles, please call:
(800) 223-1244

or visit our website at:
gale.com/thorndike

To share your comments, please write:
Publisher
Thorndike Press
10 Water St., Suite 310
Waterville, ME 04901